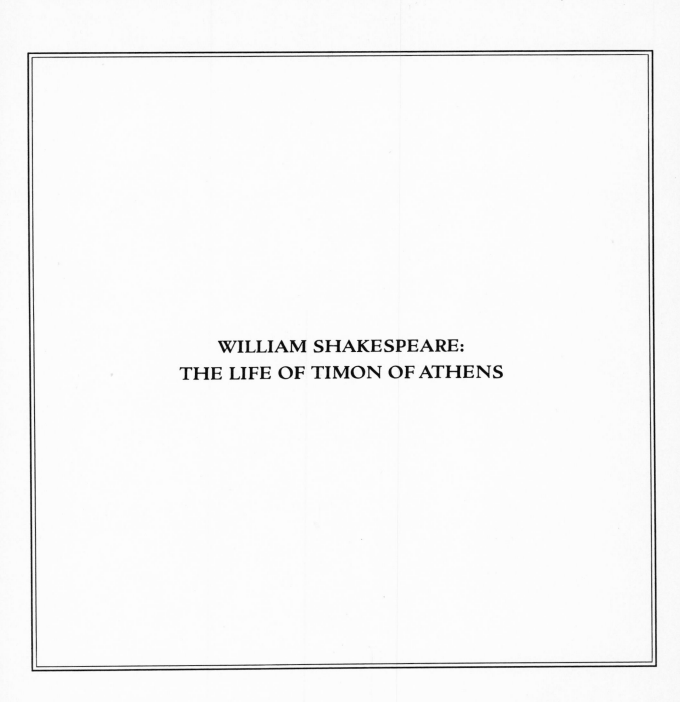

WILLIAM SHAKESPEARE:
THE LIFE OF TIMON OF ATHENS

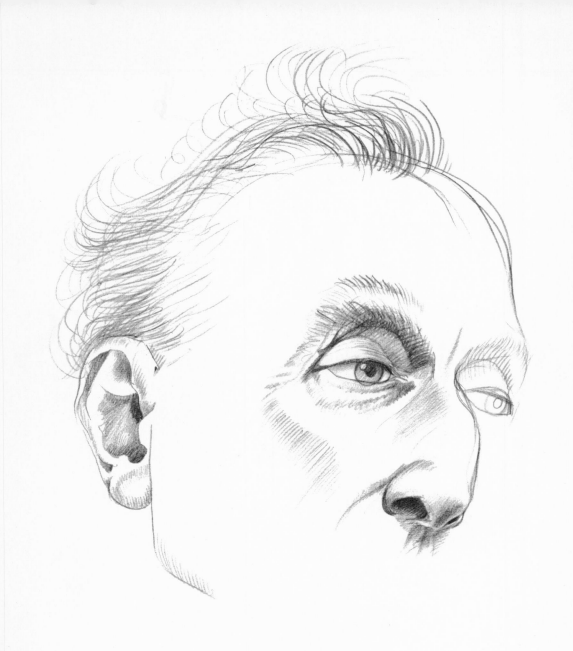

TIMON
OF ATHENS

By WILLIAM SHAKESPEARE

DESIGN BY DANIEL HABERMAN
ILLUSTRATIONS BY ISADORE SELTZER

PUBLISHED BY
RAE PUBLISHING CO., INC.
ROYAL COMPOSING ROOM, INC.
FINCH, PRUYN & COMPANY, INC.
A. HOROWITZ & SONS

INTRODUCTION—*Never mind was to be so unwise to be so kind*

Timon of Athens, by William Shakespeare, is the sixteenth in a series of annual Shakespearean keepsakes prepared for friends of the publishers.

The Life of Timon of Athens is a late, though unfinished, play (1608). The poet would subsequently devote himself to the writing of romances; and, with the exception of *The Tempest,* all of his major works had been written.
This play is one of passion.

William Hazlitt has suggested that "If poetry is a dream, the business of life is much the same…Poetry is the language of the imagination and the passions. It relates to whatever gives immediate pleasure or pain to the human mind. It comes home to the bosoms and businesses of men; for nothing but what so comes home to them in the most general and intelligible shape can be a subject for poetry. Poetry is the universal language which the heart holds with nature and itself. He who has a contempt for poetry cannot have much respect for himself, or for anything else. It is not a mere frivolous accomplishment (as some persons have been led to imagine), the trifling amusement of a few idle readers or leisure hours—it has been the study and delight of mankind in all ages…the vain, the ambitious, the proud, the choleric man, the hero and the coward, the beggar and the king, the rich and the poor, the young and the old, all live in a world of their own making; and the poet does no more than describe what all the others think and act. If his art is folly and madness, it is folly and madness at secondhand."

It is the fifth century B.C.

PROLOGUE—*From Timon, or the Misanthrope*
by Lucian of Samosata, second century A.D.

TIMON O genial, hospitable, sociable, domestic Jove, presider over oaths, cloud-masser, thunderer, lightning-sender, and by whatever other name you are given by lunatic poets, especially when they need help in their verses (because then with the multitude of your names you sustain the drooping verse and supply the lack of a rhyme), where now is your pealing thunder, your piercing lightning, and your terrible burning arrow? All these have already become fables, truly a poetic mist, where there is nothing but a parade of words. Your weapons, which once where ever-ready and wounded at a great distance, are now, I don't know how, quite extinct, and so cold that there remains in you no spark of anger against evildoers. Wherefore anyone who wished to perjure himself would be more afraid of a stinking lantern-wick than of the flame of your thunderbolt, which once awed all the world; for it seems that you direct against them nothing more than an ember without smoke and flame, from which they fear no other wound than to be dirtied with soot...

JOVE Who is that, Mercury, shouting in such a loud voice from Athenian soil under the roots of Mount Hymettus, all dirty, unkempt and dreary? He seems to have his head bent low, digging the earth. A man of many words and audacious. Perhaps he's a philosopher? For otherwise he would not speak so bitterly against us.

MERCURY What, father! Don't you recognize Timon, the son of Echecratides the Collytan? This is the man who used to invite us to complete and perfect sacrifices, and only a short time ago was rich and sacrificed hecatombs at your festival.

JOVE Alas, what a change from that fine rich man surrounded by so many friends! What has happened to him that he has become so filthy, wretched, a digger of the earth, working for pay apparently, since he's carrying in his hand such a heavy mattock?

MERCURY He was brought to this by his bounty, humanity and compassion towards all in want; or rather, to speak more correctly, by his ignorance, foolish habits, and small judgement of men, not realizing that he was giving his property to ravens and wolves. Even while the poor wretch was having his liver eaten by so many vultures, he thought they were his friends and well-wishers, who took pleasure in consuming it because of the love they bore him. When they had finally eaten him down to the bone, and sucked the marrow, they left him dry and stripped from top to toe, and now they no longer know him or condescend to look at him, or give him any help. That's why you see him in skins, with a hoe, having abandoned the city out of shame, tilling the soil in order to live, and afflicting himself when he thinks that those who have become rich through his kindnesses now despise him and do not even care to know if he is called Timon.

JOVE Truly this man does not deserve to be despised and neglected, for the poor fellow complains with good cause. We should be like those scoundrelly flatterers if we forgot him who to honour us has burned on our altars so many legs of bulls and fine fat goats, so that I still have the scent of the flesh in my nostrils.

But owning to my busyness and the loud tumult of perjurers and violent men and robbers, and also through fear of sacrilege—since these villains are numerous and difficult to keep under control, so that I hardly dare take my eyes off them—it is a long time since I even glanced at Attica, especially since philosophy and disputations began to occur among the Athenians, for with their fighting and shouting I have hardly been able to hear men's prayers, so that I must either sit with my ears closed, or be overwhelmed while they talk in loud voices of virtue, of incorporeal things, and other fictions. That is why I have not been able to attend to Timon, and although he is a good man I have neglected him...

RICHES I tell you, Jove, I don't want to go back to that man any more.

JOVE Why not, good Riches, when I have ordered it?

RICHES Because he has insulted me and chased me out and torn me to pieces and thrown me about as people do who toss out hot coals with their hands. Must I go back to be given over again into the hands of parasites and flatterers? Send me, Jove, to those who will feel gratitude for the gift, and esteem it, who care about me and desire me, and let those simpletons stay with Poverty who prefer her to me. Let the poor, who receive from her some skins and a pick, be contented when they earn fourpence and thoughtlessly throw away the gift of ten talents.

JOVE He'll never treat you again like that...

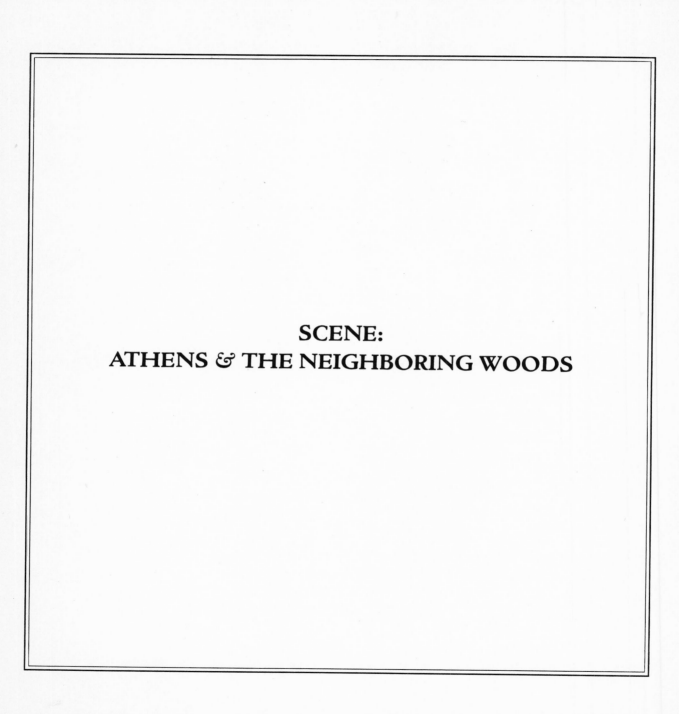

SCENE:
ATHENS & THE NEIGHBORING WOODS

DRAMATIS PERSONAE

TIMON, *a lord of Athens*
VENTIDIUS, *false friend to Timon*
APEMANTUS, *a churlish philosopher*
ALCIBIADES, *an Athenian captain*
FLAVIUS, *steward to Timon*
LUCIUS, *a flattering lord*
SEMPRONIUS, *a flattering lord*
LUCULLUS, *a flattering lord*
FLAMINIUS, SERVILIUS, LUCILIUS, *servants to Timon*
CAPHIS, PHILOTUS, TITUS, HORTENSIUS, *servants to usurers*
PHRYNIA, TIMANDRA, *mistresses to Alcibiades*
CERTAIN MASKERS, *as Cupid and Amazons*
POET, PAINTER, JEWELER,
MERCHANT, FOOL, SENATORS, LORDS,
OFFICERS, SOLDIERS, THIEVES, AND OTHERS

ACT ONE

ATHENS. TIMON'S HOUSE

[*Enter Poet, Painter, Jeweler, Merchant at several doors*]

Poet.   Good day, sir.

Painter.   I am glad y'are well.

Poet.   I have not seen you long; how goes the world?

Painter.   It wears, sir, as it grows.

Poet.   Ay that's well known.
But what particular rarity? What strange,
Which manifold record not matches? See,
Magic of bounty, all these spirits thy power
Hath conjured to attend. I know the merchant.

Painter.   I know them both; th' other's a jeweler.

Merchant.   O 'tis a worthy lord.

Jeweler.   Nay that's most fixed.

Merchant.   A most incomparable man, breathed, as it were,
To an untirable and continuate goodness.
He passes.

Jeweler.   I have a jewel here —

Merchant.   O pray let's see't. For the Lord Timon, sir?

Jeweler.   If he will touch the estimate. But for that—

Poet.   [*Aside to Painter*] When we for recompense have praised the vild,
It stains the glory in that happy verse
Which aptly sings the good.

Merchant.   [*Looking at the jewel*] 'Tis a good form.

Jeweler.   And rich. Here is a water, look ye.

Painter.   You are rapt, sir, in some work, some dedication
To the great lord.

Poet.   A thing slipped idly from me.
Our poesy is as a gum, which oozes
From whence 'tis nourished. The fire i' th' flint
Shows not till it be struck; our gentle flame
Provokes itself, and like the current flies
Each bound it chases. What have you there?

Painter.   A picture, sir. When comes your book forth?

Poet.   Upon the heels of my presentment, sir.
Let's see your piece.

Painter.   'Tis a good piece.

Poet.   So 'tis; this comes off well and excellent.

Painter.   Indifferent.

Poet.　　　　　　　　　　Admirable. How this grace
　　　　　Speaks his own standing! What a mental power
　　　　　This eye shoots forth! How big imagination
　　　　　Moves in this lip! To th' dumbness of the gesture
　　　　　One might interpret.
Painter.　　It is a pretty mocking of the life.
　　　　　Here is a touch—is't good?
Poet.　　　　　　　　　　　　　　　I will say of it,
　　　　　It tutors nature; artificial strife
　　　　　Lives in these touches, livelier than life.
　　　　　　　[*Enter certain Senators, who pass over the stage and exeunt*]
Painter.　　How this lord is followed!
Poet.　　　The senators of Athens, happy men!
Painter.　　Look, moe!
Poet.　　　You see this confluence, this great flood of visitors:
　　　　　I have in this rough work shaped out a man
　　　　　Whom this beneath world doth embrace and hug
　　　　　With amplest entertainment. My free drift
　　　　　Halts not particularly, but moves itself
　　　　　In a wide sea of wax; no leveled malice

Infects one comma in the course I hold,
But flies an eagle flight, bold and forth on,
Leaving no tract behind.

Painter. How shall I understand you?

Poet.   I will unbolt to you.
You see how all conditions, how all minds,
As well of glib and slipp'ry creatures as
Of grave and austere quality, tender down
Their services to Lord Timon. His large fortune,
Upon his good and gracious nature hanging,
Subdues and properties to his love and tendance
All sorts of hearts; yea, from the glass-faced flatterer
To Apemantus, that few things loves better
Than to abhor himself—even he drops down
The knee before him, and returns in peace
Most rich in Timon's nod.

Painter.   I saw them speak together.

Poet. Sir, I have upon a high and pleasant hill
Feigned Fortune to be throned. The base o' th' mount
Is ranked with all deserts, all kind of natures

That labor on the bosom of this sphere
To propagate their states. Amongst them all,
Whose eyes are on this sovereign lady fixed,
One do I personate of Lord Timon's frame,
Whom Fortune with her ivory hand wafts to her,
Whose present grace to present slaves and servants
Translates his rivals.

Painter.   'Tis conceived to scope.
This throne, this Fortune, and this hill, methinks,
With one man beckoned from the rest below,
Bowing his head against the steepy mount
To climb his happiness, would be well expressed
In our condition.

Poet.   Nay, sir, but hear me on.
All those which were his fellows but of late,
Some better than his value, on the moment
Follow his strides, his lobbies fill with tendance,
Rain sacrificial whisperings in his ear,
Make sacred even his stirrup, and through him
Drink the free air.

Painter.   Ay marry, what of these?

Poet.   When Fortune in her shift and change of mood
Spurns down her late beloved, all his dependants
Which labored after him to the mountain's top,
Even on their knees and hands, let him slip down,
Not one accompanying his declining foot.

Painter. 'Tis common.
A thousand moral paintings I can show
That shall demonstrate these quick blows of Fortune's
More pregnantly than words. Yet you do well
To show Lord Timon that mean eyes have seen
The foot above the head.

        [*Trumpets sound. Enter Lord Timon, addressing himself
        courteously to every suitor; a Messenger from Ventidius
        talking with him; Lucilius and other servants following*]

Timon.   Imprisoned is he, say you?

Messenger. Ay, my good lord; five talents is his debt,
His means most short, his creditors most strait.
Your honorable letter he desires
To those have shut him up, which failing,

Periods his comfort.

Timon.   Noble Ventidius—well.
I am not of that feather to shake off
My friend when he must need me. I do know him
A gentleman that well deserves a help,
Which he shall have. I'll pay the debt and free him.

Messenger. Your lordship ever binds him.

Timon. Commend me to him; I will send his ransom,
And being enfranchised bid him come to me.
'Tis not enough to help the feeble up,
But to support him after. Fare you well.

Messenger. All happiness to your honor.

           [*Exit*]

           [*Enter an Old Athenian*]

Old Athenian. Lord Timon, hear me speak.

Timon.   Freely, good father.

Old Athenian. Thou hast a servant named Lucilius.

Timon. I have so. What of him?

Old Athenian. Most noble Timon, call the man before thee.

Timon. Attends he here or no? Lucilius!

Lucilius.	Here at your lordship's service.
Old Athenian.	This fellow here, Lord Timon, this thy creature,
	By night frequents my house. I am a man
	That from my first have been inclined to thrift,
	And my estate deserves an heir more raised
	Than one which holds a trencher.
Timon.	Well; what further?
Old Athenian.	One only daughter have I, no kin else,
	On whom I may confer what I have got.
	The maid is fair, a th' youngest for a bride,
	And I have bred her at my dearest cost
	In qualities of the best. This man of thine
	Attempts her love. I prithee, noble lord,
	Join with me to forbid him her resort;
	Myself have spoke in vain.
Timon.	The man is honest.
Old Athenian.	Therefore he will be, Timon.
	His honesty rewards him in itself;
	It must not bear my daughter.
Timon.	Does she love him?

Old Athenian.   She is young and apt.
       Our own precedent passions do instruct us
       What levity's in youth.

Timon.   Love you the maid?

Lucilius.   Ay, my good lord, and she accepts of it.

Old Athenian.   If in her marriage my consent be missing,
       I call the gods to witness, I will choose
       Mine heir from forth the beggars of the world,
       And dispossess her all.

Timon.   How shall she be endowed,
       If she be mated with an equal husband?

Old Athenian.   Three talents on the present; in future, all.

Timon.   This gentleman of mine hath served me long.
       To build his fortune I will strain a little,
       For 'tis a bond in men. Give him thy daughter;
       What you bestow, in him I'll counterpoise,
       And make him weigh with her.

Old Athenian.   Most noble lord,
       Pawn me to this your honor, she is his.

Timon.   My hand to thee, mine honor on my promise.

Lucilius.   Humbly I thank your lordship; never may
That state or fortune fall into my keeping,
Which is not owed to you.

              [Exit Lucilius, with Old Athenian]

Poet.   Vouchsafe my labor, and long live your lordship.

Timon.   I thank you; you shall hear from me anon.
Go not away. What have you there, my friend?

Painter.   A piece of painting, which I do beseech
Your lordship to accept.

Timon.   Painting is welcome.
The painting is almost the natural man;
For since dishonor traffics with man's nature,
He is but outside. These penciled figures are
Even such as they give out. I like your work,
And you shall find I like it. Wait attendance
Till you hear further from me.

Painter.   The gods preserve ye.

Timon.   Well fare you, gentleman. Give me your hand;
We must needs dine together. Sir, your jewel
Hath suffered under praise.

Jeweler.   What, my lord, dispraise?

Timon.   A mere satiety of commendations.
If I should pay you for't as 'tis extolled,
It would unclew me quite.

Jeweler.   My lord, 'tis rated
As those which sell would give. But you well know,
Things of like value, differing in the owners,
Are prizèd by their masters. Believe't, dear lord,
You mend the jewel by the wearing it.

Timon.   Well mocked.

Merchant.   No, my good lord; he speaks the common tongue
Which all men speak with him.

                  [*Enter Apemantus*]

Timon.   Look who comes here; will you be chid?

Jeweler.   We'll bear with your lordship.

Merchant.   He'll spare none.

Timon.   Good morrow to thee, gentle Apemantus.

Apemantus.   Till I be gentle, stay thou for thy good morrow—
When thou art Timon's dog, and these knaves honest.

Timon.   Why dost thou call them knaves, thou know'st them not?

Apemantus.	Are they not Athenians?
Timon.	Yes.
Apemantus.	Then I repent not.
Jeweler.	You know me, Apemantus?
Apemantus.	Thou know'st I do, I called thee by thy name.
Timon.	Thou art proud, Apemantus.
Apemantus.	Of nothing so much as that I am not like Timon.
Timon.	Whither art going?
Apemantus.	To knock out an honest Athenian's brains.
Timon.	That's a deed thou't die for.
Apemantus.	Right, if doing nothing be death by th' law.
Timon.	How lik'st thou this picture, Apemantus?
Apemantus.	The best, for the innocence.
Timon.	Wrought he not well that painted it?
Apemantus.	He wrought better that made the painter, and yet he's but a filthy piece of work.
Painter.	Y'are a dog.
Apemantus.	Thy mother's of my generation. What's she, if I be a dog?
Timon.	Wilt dine with me, Apemantus?
Apemantus.	No. I eat not lords.

Timon.   And thou shouldst, thou'dst anger ladies.

Apemantus.   O they eat lords; so they come by great bellies.

Timon.   That's a lascivious apprehension.

Apemantus.   So, thou apprehend'st it, take it for thy labor.

Timon.   How dost thou like this jewel, Apemantus?

Apemantus.   Not so well as plain-dealing, which will not cost a man a doit.

Timon.   What dost thou think 'tis worth?

Apemantus.   Not worth my thinking. How now, poet?

Poet.   How now, philosopher?

Apemantus.   Thou liest.

Poet.   Art not one?

Apemantus.   Yes.

Poet.   Then I lie not.

Apemantus.   Art not a poet?

Poet.   Yes.

Apemantus.   Then thou liest. Look in thy last work, where thou hast feigned him a worthy fellow.

Poet.   That's not feigned, he is so.

Apemantus.   Yes, he is worthy of thee, and to pay thee for thy labor. He that loves to be flattered is worthy o' th'

	flatterer. Heavens, that I were a lord!
Timon.	What wouldst do then, Apemantus?
Apemantus.	E'en as Apemantus does now: hate a lord with my heart.
Timon.	What, thyself?
Apemantus.	Ay.
Timon.	Wherefore?
Apemantus.	That I had no angry wit to be a lord. Art not thou a merchant?
Merchant.	Ay, Apemantus.
Apemantus.	Traffic confound thee, if the gods will not.
Merchant.	If traffic do it, the gods do it.
Apemantus.	Traffic's thy god, and thy god confound thee.

[Trumpet sounds. Enter a Messenger]

Timon.	What trumpet's that?
Messenger.	'Tis Alcibiades and some twenty horse,
	All of companionship.
Timon.	Pray entertain them, give them guide to us.

[Exeunt some Attendants]

You must needs dine with me. Go not you hence
Till I have thanked you. When dinner's done
Show me this piece. I am joyful of your sights.

[Enter Alcibiades with the rest]

Most welcome, sir.

Apemantus.   So, so.

Their aches contract and starve your supple joints!
That there should be small love amongst these sweet knaves,
And all this courtesy! The strain of man's bred out
Into baboon and monkey.

Alcibiades.   Sir, you have saved my longing, and I feed
Most hungerly on your sight.

Timon.   Right welcome, sir.

Ere we depart, we'll share a bounteous time
In different pleasures. Pray you let us in.

[Exeunt all but Apemantus]

[Enter two Lords]

First Lord.   What time a day is't, Apemantus?

Apemantus.   Time to be honest.

First Lord.   That time serves still.

Apemantus.   The most accursèd thou that still omit'st it.

Second Lord.   Thou art going to Lord Timon's feast?

Apemantus.   Ay, to see meat fill knaves and wine heat fools.

Second Lord.	Fare thee well, fare thee well.
Apemantus.	Thou art a fool to bid me farewell twice.
Second Lord.	Why, Apemantus?
Apemantus.	Shouldst have kept one to thyself, for I mean to give thee none.
First Lord.	Hang thyself!
Apemantus.	No, I will do nothing at thy bidding.
	Make thy requests to thy friend.
Second Lord.	Away, unpeaceable dog, or I'll spurn thee hence.
Apemantus.	I will fly like a dog the heels a th' ass.
	[Exit]
First Lord.	He's opposite to humanity. Come, shall we in
	And taste Lord Timon's bounty? He outgoes
	The very heart of kindness.
Second Lord.	He pours it out. Plutus, the god of gold,
	Is but his steward; no meed but he repays
	Sevenfold above itself. No gift to him
	But breeds the giver a return exceeding
	All use of quittance.
First Lord.	The noblest mind he carries
	That ever governed man.

Second Lord.   Long may he live
In fortunes. Shall we in?
First Lord.   I'll keep you company.
     [*Exeunt*]

TIMON'S HOUSE

[Hautboys playing loud music. A great banquet served in; and then enter
Lord Timon, the States, the Athenian Lords, Ventidius (which Timon
redeemed from prison), and Alcibiades. Steward and others attending.
Then comes dropping after all, Apemantus, discontentedly, like himself]

Ventidius.   Most honored Timon,
        It hath pleased the gods to remember my father's age,
        And call him to long peace.
        He is gone happy, and has left me rich.
        Then, as in grateful virtue I am bound
        To your free heart, I do return those talents
        Doubled with thanks and service, from whose help
        I derived liberty.

Timon.   O by no means,
        Honest Ventidius. You mistake my love;
        I gave it freely ever, and there's none
        Can truly say he gives, if he receives.
        If our betters play at that game, we must not dare
        To imitate them; faults that are rich are fair.

Ventidius.   A noble spirit.

Timon.   Nay, my lords, ceremony was but devised at first
To set a gloss on faint deeds, hollow welcomes,
Recanting goodness, sorry ere 'tis shown.
But where there is true friendship, there needs none.
Pray sit; more welcome are ye to my fortunes
Than my fortunes to me.

First Lord.   My lord, we always have confessed it.

Apemantus.   Ho, ho, confessed it? Hanged it, have you not?

Timon.   O Apemantus, you are welcome.

Apemantus.   No, you shall not make me welcome.
I come to have thee thrust me out of doors.

Timon.   Fie, th'art a churl, y'have got a humor there
Does not become a man; 'tis much to blame.
They say, my lords, *Ira furor brevis est,* but yond man
is ever angry. Go, let him have a table by himself, for
he does neither affect company, nor is he fit for't
indeed.

Apemantus.   Let me stay at thine apperil, Timon. I come to
observe, I give thee warning on't.

Timon. I take no heed of thee. Th'art an Athenian, therefore welcome. I myself would have no power;
prithee let my meat make thee silent.

Apemantus. I scorn thy meat; 'twould choke me, for I should
ne'er flatter thee. O you gods! What a number of
men eats Timon, and he sees 'em not! It grieves me
to see so many dip their meat in one man's blood,
and all the madness is, he cheers them up too.
I wonder men dare trust themselves with men.
Methinks they should invite them without knives:
Good for their meat, and safer for their lives.
There's much example for't; the fellow that sits next
him, now parts bread with him, pledges the breath
of him in a divided draught, is the readiest man to
kill him. 'T'as been proved. If I were a huge man, I
should fear to drink at meals,
Lest they should spy my windpipe's dangerous notes;
Great men should drink with harness on their throats.

Timon. My lord, in heart; and let the health go round.

Second Lord. Let it flow this way, my good lord.

Apemantus. Flow this way? A brave fellow. He keeps his tides well. Those
healths will make thee and thy state look ill, Timon.
Here's that which is too weak to be a sinner,
Honest water, which ne'er left man i' th' mire.
This and my food are equals, there's no odds;
Feasts are too proud to give thanks to the gods.

　　　[Apemantus' Grace]
　　　　Immortal gods, I crave no pelf;
　　　　I pray for no man but myself.
　　　　Grant I may never prove so fond
　　　　To trust man on his oath or bond,
　　　　Or a harlot for her weeping,
　　　　Or a dog that seems a-sleeping,
　　　　Or a keeper with my freedom,
　　　　Or my friends if I should need 'em.
　　　　Amen. So fall to't:
Rich men sin, and I eat root. *[Eats and drinks]*
Much good dich thy good heart, Apemantus.

Timon. Captain Alcibiades, your heart's in the field now.

Alcibiades. My heart is ever at your service, my lord.

Timon.   You had rather be at a breakfast of enemies than a dinner of friends.

Alcibiades.   So they were bleeding new, my lord, there's no meat like 'em; I could wish my best friend at such a feast.

Apemantus.   Would all those flatterers were thine enemies then, that then thou mightst kill 'em—and bid me to 'em.

First Lord.   Might we but have that happiness, my lord, that you would once use our hearts, whereby we might express some part of our zeals, we should think ourselves for ever perfect.

Timon.   O no doubt, my good friends, but the gods themselves have provided that I shall have much help from you: how had you been my friends else? Why have you that charitable title from thousands, did not you chiefly belong to my heart? I have told more of you to myself than you can with modesty speak in your own behalf; and thus far I confirm you. O you gods, think I, what need we have any friends, if we should ne'er have need of 'em? They were the most needless creatures living should we

ne'er have use for 'em, and would most resemble
sweet instruments hung up in cases, that keeps their
sounds to themselves. Why I have often wished
myself poorer that I might come nearer to you. We
are born to do benefits; and what better or properer
can we call our own than the riches of our friends?
O what a precious comfort 'tis to have so many like
brothers commanding one another's fortunes. O
joy's e'en made away ere't can be born. Mine eyes
cannot hold out water, methinks. To forget their
faults, I drink to you.

Apemantus. Thou weep'st to make them drink, Timon.

Second Lord. Joy had the like conception in our eyes,
And at that instant like a babe sprung up.

Apemantus. Ho, ho! I laugh to think that babe a bastard.

Third Lord. I promise you, my lord, you moved me much.

Apemantus. Much.

[*Sound tucket*]

Timon. What means that trump?

[*Enter Servant*]

                     How now?

Servant.   Please you, my lord, there are certain ladies most
desirous of admittance.

Timon.   Ladies? What are their wills?

Servant.   There comes with them a forerunner, my lord, which
bears that office to signify their pleasures.

Timon.   I pray let them be admitted.

       [*Enter Cupid*]

Cupid.   Hail to thee, worthy Timon, and to all
That of his bounties taste. The five best senses
Acknowledge thee their patron, and come freely
To gratulate thy plenteous bosom. Th' ear,
Taste, touch, all, pleased from thy table rise;
They only now come but to feast thine eyes.

Timon.   They're welcome all; let 'em have kind admittance.
Music make their welcome.

       [*Exit Cupid*]

First Lord.   You see, my lord, how ample y'are beloved.

       [*Music. Enter Cupid with the Masque of Ladies as
Amazons, with lutes in their hands, dancing and playing*]

Apemantus.   Hoy-day!

What a sweep of vanity comes this way.

They dance? They are madwomen.

Like madness is the glory of this life,

As this pomp shows to a little oil and root.

We make ourselves fools to disport ourselves,

And spend our flatteries to drink those men

Upon whose age we void it up again

With poisonous spite and envy.

Who lives that's not depravèd or depraves?

Who dies that bears not one spurn to their graves

Of their friends' gift?

I should fear those that dance before me now

Would one day stamp upon me. 'T'as been done.

Men shut their doors against a setting sun.

     [*The Lords rise from table, with much adoring*

     of Timon, and to show their loves, each single

     out an Amazon, and all dance, men with women,

     a lofty strain or two to the hautboys, and cease]

Timon.   You have done our pleasures much grace, fair ladies,

Set a fair fashion on our entertainment,
Which was not half so beautiful and kind.
You have added worth unto't and luster,
And entertained me with mine own device.
I am to thank you for't.

First Lady. My lord, you take us even at the best.

Apemantus. Faith, for the worst is filthy, and would not hold taking,
I doubt me.

Timon. Ladies, there is an idle banquet attends you,
Please you to dispose yourselves.

All Ladies. Most thankfully, my lord.

                    [*Exeunt Cupid and Ladies*]

Timon. Flavius.

Flavius. My lord.

Timon.   The little casket bring me hither.

Flavius. Yes, my lord.

[*Aside*] More jewels yet?
There is no crossing him in's humor,
Else I should tell him well, i' faith I should,
When all's spent, he'd be crossed then, and he could.

'Tis pity bounty had not eyes behind,
That man might ne'er be wretched for his mind.
      [Exit]

First Lord. Where be our men?

Servant. Here, my lord, in readiness.

Second Lord. Our horses.
      [Enter Flavius with the casket]

Timon. O my friends,
I have one word to say to you. Look you, my good lord,
I must entreat you honor me so much
As to advance this jewel; accept it and wear it,
Kind my lord.

First Lord. I am so far already in your gifts —

All. So are we all.
      [Enter a Servant]

Servant. My lord, there are certain nobles of the senate newly
alighted, and come to visit you.

Timon. They are fairly welcome.

Flavius. I beseech your honor, vouchsafe me a word;
it does concern you near.

Timon.   Near? Why then another time I'll hear thee. I prithee let's be
          provided to show them entertainment.

Flavius. [Aside]   I scarce know how.

          [Enter another Servant]

Second Servant.   May it please your honor, Lord Lucius,
          Out of his free love, hath presented to you
          Four milk-white horses, trapped in silver.

Timon.   I shall accept them fairly. Let the presents
          Be worthily entertained.

          [Enter a third Servant]

                                   How now? What news?

Third Servant.   Please you, my lord, that honorable gentleman Lord
          Lucullus entreats your company tomorrow to hunt
          with him, and has sent your honor two brace of
          greyhounds.

Timon.   I'll hunt with him, and let them be received
          Not without fair reward.

Flavius. [Aside]   What will this come to?
          He commands us to provide, and give great gifts,
          And all out of an empty coffer;

Nor will he know his purse, or yield me this,
To show him what a beggar his heart is,
Being of no power to make his wishes good.
His promises fly so beyond his state
That what he speaks is all in debt; he owes for ev'ry word.
He is so kind that he now pays interest for't;
His land's put to their books. Well, would I were
Gently put out of office before I were forced out.
Happier is he that has no friend to feed
Than such that do e'en enemies exceed.
I bleed inwardly for my lord.
                    [*Exit*]

Timon.   You do yourselves much wrong,
You bate too much of your own merits.
Here, my lord, a trifle of our love.

Second Lord.   With more than common thanks I will receive it.

Third Lord.   O he's the very soul of bounty.

Timon.   And now I remember, my lord, you gave good
words the other day of a bay courser I rode on. 'Tis
yours because you liked it.

First Lord.	O I beseech you pardon me, my lord, in that.
Timon.	You may take my word, my lord, I know no man can
	justly praise but what he does affect. I weigh my
	friend's affection with mine own. I'll tell you true,
	I'll call to you.
All Lords.	O none so welcome.
Timon.	I take all and your several visitations
	So kind to heart, 'tis not enough to give.
	Methinks I could deal kingdoms to my friends,
	And ne'er be weary. Alcibiades,
	Thou art a soldier, therefore seldom rich;
	It comes in charity to thee, for all thy living
	Is 'mongst the dead, and all the lands thou hast
	Lie in a pitched field.
Alcibiades.	Ay, defiled land, my lord.
First Lord.	We are so virtuously bound—
Timon.	And so am I to you.
Second Lord.	So infinitely endeared—
Timon.	All to you. Lights, more lights!
First Lord.	The best of happiness, honor, and fortunes

Keep with you, Lord Timon.

Timon. Ready for his friends.

　　[Exeunt Lords]

Apemantus. 　　　　　　　　What a coil's here,
Serving of becks and jutting out of bums!
I doubt whether their legs be worth the sums
That are given for 'em. Friendship's full of dregs;
Methinks false hearts should never have sound legs.
Thus honest fools lay out their wealth on curtsies.

Timon. Now Apemantus, if thou wert not sullen,
I would be good to thee.

Apemantus. No, I'll nothing; for if I should be bribed too, there
would be none left to rail upon thee, and then thou
wouldst sin the faster. Thou giv'st so long, Timon, I
fear me thou wilt give away thyself in paper shortly.
What needs these feasts, pomps, and vainglories?

Timon. Nay, and you begin to rail on society once, I am
sworn not to give regard to you. Farewell, and come
with better music.

　　[Exit]

Apemantus. So. Thou wilt not hear me now, thou shalt not then.
I'll lock thy heaven from thee.
O that men's ears should be
To counsel deaf, but not to flattery.
      [*Exit*]

ACT TWO

A SENATOR'S HOUSE

[Enter a Senator]

Senator. And late five thousand. To Varro and to Isidore
He owes nine thousand, besides my former sum,
Which makes it five and twenty. Still in motion
Of raging waste? It cannot hold, it will not.
If I want gold, steal but a beggar's dog
And give it Timon—why the dog coins gold.
If I would sell my horse and buy twenty moe
Better than he—why give my horse to Timon;
Ask nothing, give it him, it foals me straight,
And able horses. No porter at his gate,
But rather one that smiles, and still invites
All that pass by. It cannot hold; no reason
Can sound his state in safety. Caphis, ho!
Caphis, I say!
                  [Enter Caphis]

Caphis.   Here, sir, what is your pleasure?
Senator. Get on your cloak, and haste you to Lord Timon;

Importune him for my moneys; be not ceased
With slight denial; nor then silenced when
"Commend me to your master" and the cap
Plays in the right hand, thus—but tell him,
My uses cry to me; I must serve my turn
Out of mine own; his days and times are past,
And my reliances on his fracted dates
Have smit my credit. I love and honor him,
But must not break my back to heal his finger.
Immediate are my needs, and my relief
Must not be tossed and turned to me in words,
But find supply immediate. Get you gone;
Put on a most importunate aspect,
A visage of demand; for I do fear,
When every feather sticks in his own wing,
Lord Timon will be left a naked gull,
Which flashes now a phoenix. Get you gone.

Caphis.   I go, sir.
Senator.   Ay, go sir! Take the bonds along with you,
And have the dates in. Come!

Caphis.   I will, sir.

Senator.   Go!

[*Exeunt*]

TIMON'S HOUSE

[Enter Flavius, the Steward,
with many bills in his hand]

Flavius.   No care, no stop, so senseless of expense

That he will neither know how to maintain it,

Nor cease his flow of riot. Takes no accompt

How things go from him, nor resumes no care

Of what is to continue. Never mind

Was to be so unwise to be so kind.

What shall be done he will not hear, till feel.

I must be round with him, now he comes from hunting.

Fie, fie, fie, fie!

[Enter Caphis, with the Servants of Isidore and Varro]

Caphis.   Good even, Varro. What, you come for money?

Varro's Servant.   Is't not your business too?

Caphis.   It is; and yours too, Isidore?

Isidore's Servant.   It is so.

Caphis.   Would we were all discharged.

Varro's Servant.   I fear it.

Caphis.   Here comes the lord.

             [*Enter Timon and his Train, and Alcibiades*]

Timon.   So soon as dinner's done, we'll forth again,

        My Alcibiades.

        [*To Caphis*]   With me, what is your will?

Caphis.   My lord, here is a note of certain dues.

Timon.   Dues? Whence are you?

Caphis.   Of Athens here, my lord.

Timon.   Go to my steward.

Caphis.   Please it your lordship, he hath put me off

        To the succession of new days this month.

        My master is awaked by great occasion

        To call upon his own, and humbly prays you

        That with your other noble parts you'll suit

        In giving him his right.

Timon.   Mine honest friend,

        I prithee but repair to me next morning.

Caphis.   Nay, good my lord—

Timon.   Contain thyself, good friend.

Varro's Servant.   One Varro's servant, my good lord—

Isidore's Servant. From Isidore; he humbly prays your speedy payment.

Caphis. If you did know, my lord, my master's wants —

Varro's Servant. 'Twas due on forfeiture, my lord, six weeks and past.

Isidore's Servant. Your steward puts me off, my lord,
and I am sent expressly to your lordship.

Timon. Give me breath.
I do beseech you, good my lords, keep on;
I'll wait upon you instantly.

    [Exeunt Alcibiades and Lords]

    [To Flavius]

                    Come hither. Pray you,
How goes the world, that I am thus encount'red
With clamorous demands of broken bonds,
And the detention of long since due debts
Against my honor?

Flavius.   Please you, gentlemen,
The time is unagreeable to this business.
Your importunacy cease till after dinner,
That I may make his lordship understand
Wherefore you are not paid.

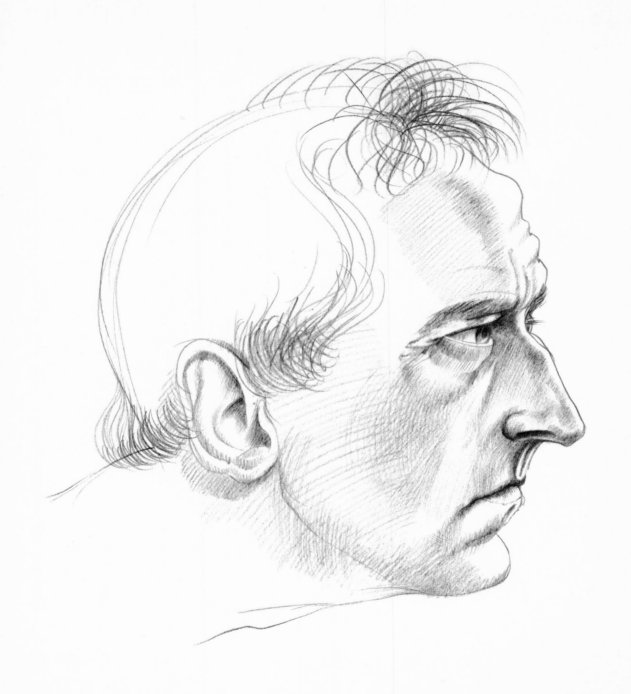

Timon.	Do so, my friends. See them well entertained.
	[Exit]
Flavius.	Pray draw near.
	[Exit]
	[Enter Apemantus and Fool]
Caphis.	Stay, stay, here comes the fool with Apemantus.
	Let's ha' some sport with 'em.
Varro's Servant.	Hang him, he'll abuse us.
Isidore's Servant.	A plague upon him, dog!
Varro's Servant.	How dost, fool?
Apemantus.	Dost dialogue with thy shadow?
Varro's Servant.	I speak not to thee.
Apemantus.	No, 'tis to thyself. *[To the Fool]* Come away.
Isidore's Servant.	*[To Varro's Servant]* There's the fool hangs on your back already.
Apemantus.	No, thou stand'st single, th'art not on him yet.
Caphis.	Where's the fool now?
Apemantus.	He last asked the question. Poor rogues and
	usurers' men, bawds between gold and want.
All Servants.	What are we, Apemantus?
Apemantus.	Asses.

All Servants.	Why?
Apemantus.	That you ask me what you are, and do not know yourselves. Speak to 'em, fool.
Fool.	How do you, gentlemen?
All Servants.	Gramercies, good fool. How does your mistress?
Fool.	She's e'en setting on water to scald such chickens as you are. Would we could see you at Corinth.
Apemantus.	Good, gramercy.

[Enter Page]

Fool.	Look you, here comes my mistress' page.
Page.	*[To the Fool]* Why, how now, captain? What do you in this wise company? How dost thou, Apemantus?
Apemantus.	Would I had a rod in my mouth, that I might answer thee profitably.
Page.	Prithee, Apemantus, read me the superscription of these letters. I know not which is which.
Apemantus.	Canst not read?
Page.	No.
Apemantus.	There will little learning die then that day thou art hanged. This is to Lord Timon, this to Alcibiades.

Go, thou wast born a bastard, and thou'lt die a bawd.

Page. Thou wast whelped a dog, and thou shalt famish a dog's death. Answer not, I am gone.

    [*Exit*]

Apemantus. E'en so thou outrun'st grace. Fool, I will go with you to Lord Timon's.

Fool. Will you leave me there?

Apemantus. If Timon stay at home. You three serve three usurers?

All Servants. Ay; would they served us.

Apemantus. So would I—as good a trick as ever hangman served thief.

Fool. Are you three usurers' men?

All Servants. Ay, fool.

Fool. I think no usurer but has a fool to his servant. My mistress is one, and I am her fool. When men come to borrow of your masters, they approach sadly, and go away merry; but they enter my mistress' house merrily, and go away sadly. The reason of this?

Varro's Servant. I could render one.

Apemantus.	Do it then, that we may account thee a whoremaster and a knave, which notwithstanding, thou shalt be no less esteemed.
Varro's Servant.	What is a whoremaster, fool?
Fool.	A fool in good clothes, and something like thee. 'Tis a spirit; sometime't appears like a lord, sometime like a lawyer, sometime like a philosopher, with two stones moe than's artificial one. He is very often like a knight; and generally, in all shapes that man goes up and down in, from fourscore to thirteen, this spirit walks in.
Varro's Servant.	Thou are not altogether a fool.
Fool.	Nor thou altogether a wise man. As much foolery as I have, so much wit thou lack'st.
Apemantus.	That answer might have become Apemantus.
	[*Enter Timon and Flavius, the Steward*]
All Servants.	Aside, aside, here comes Lord Timon.
Apemantus.	Come with me, fool, come.
Fool.	I do not always follow lover, elder brother, and woman; sometime the philosopher.

Flavius.   Pray you, walk near: I'll speak with you anon.

            [*Exeunt Apemantus, Fool, and Servants*]

Timon.   You make me marvel wherefore ere this time

      Had you not fully laid my state before me,

      That I might so have rated my expense

      As I had leave of means.

Flavius.   You would not hear me.

      At many leisures I proposed —

Timon.   Go to.

      Perchance some single vantages you took

      When my indisposition put you back,

      And that unaptness made your minister

      Thus to excuse yourself.

Flavius.   O my good lord,

      At many times I brought in my accompts,

      Laid them before you; you would throw them off,

      And say you found them in mine honesty.

      When for some trifling present you have bid me

      Return so much, I have shook my head and wept;

      Yea 'gainst th' authority of manners, prayed you

To hold your hand more close. I did endure
Not seldom, nor no slight checks, when I have
Prompted you in the ebb of your estate
And your great flow of debts. My loved lord,
Though you hear now, too late, yet now's a time:
The greatest of your having lacks a half
To pay your present debts.

Timon.   Let all my land be sold.

Flavius. 'Tis all engaged, some forfeited and gone,
And what remains will hardly stop the mouth
Of present dues. The future comes apace.
What shall defend the interim? And at length
How goes our reck'ning?

Timon. To Lacedaemon did my land extend.

Flavius. O my good lord, the world is but a word;
Were it all yours to give it in a breath,
How quickly were it gone!

Timon.   You tell me true.

Flavius. If you suspect my husbandry or falsehood,
Call me before th' exactest auditors,

And set me on the proof. So the gods bless me,
When all our offices have been oppressed
With riotous feeders, when our vaults have wept
With drunken spilth of wine, when every room
Hath blazed with lights and brayed with minstrelsy,
I have retired me to a wasteful cock,
And set mine eyes at flow.

Timon.   Prithee no more.

Flavius.   Heavens, have I said, the bounty of this lord!
How many prodigal bits have slaves and peasants
This night englutted! Who is not Timon's?
What heart, head, sword, force, means, but is Lord Timon's?
Great Timon, noble, worthy, royal Timon!
Ah, when the means are gone that buy this praise,
The breath is gone whereof this praise is made.
Feast-won, fast-lost; one cloud of winter show'rs,
These flies are couched.

Timon.   Come, sermon me no further.
No villainous bounty yet hath passed my heart;
Unwisely, not ignobly, have I given.

Why dost thou weep? Canst thou the conscience lack
To think I shall lack friends? Secure thy heart.
If I would broach the vessels of my love,
And try the argument of hearts by borrowing,
Men and men's fortunes could I frankly use
As I can bid thee speak.

Flavius.   Assurance bless your thoughts.

Timon.   And in some sort these wants of mine are crowned,
That I account them blessings; for by these
Shall I try friends. You shall perceive how you
Mistake my fortunes; I am wealthy in my friends.
Within there! Flaminius! Servilius!

        [Enter Flaminius, Servilius, and Third Servant]

Servants.   My lord, my lord.

Timon.   I will dispatch you severally. *[To Servilius]* You to Lord
Lucius, *[to Flaminius]* to Lord Lucullus you; I hunted
with his honor today. *[To Third Servant]* You to Sempronius. Commend me to their loves; and I am proud, say,
that my occasions have found time to use 'em toward
a supply of money. Let the request be fifty talents.

Flaminius. As you have said, my lord.

  [*Exeunt Servants*]

Flavius. [*Aside*] Lord Lucius and Lucullus? Humh!

Timon. Go you, sir, to the senators,
Of whom, even to the state's best health, I have
Deserved this hearing. Bid 'em send o' th' instant
A thousand talents to me.

Flavius.   I have been bold,
For that I knew it the most general way,
To them to use your signet and your name;
But they do shake their heads, and I am here
No richer in return.

Timon.   Is't true? Can't be?

Flavius. They answer in a joint and corporate voice,
That now they are at fall, want treasure, cannot
Do what they would, are sorry; you are honorable,
But yet they could have wished—they know not;
Something hath been amiss—a noble nature
May catch a wrench—would all were well—'tis pity—
And so, intending other serious matters,

After distasteful looks, and these hard fractions,
With certain half-caps and cold-moving nods,
They froze me into silence.

Timon.   You gods reward them!
Prithee man look cheerly. These old fellows
Have their ingratitude in them hereditary.
Their blood is caked, 'tis cold, it seldom flows;
'Tis lack of kindly warmth they are not kind;
And nature, as it grows again toward earth,
Is fashioned for the journey, dull and heavy.
Go to Ventidius. Prithee be not sad;
Thou art true and honest; ingeniously I speak,
No blame belongs to thee. Ventidius lately
Buried his father, by whose death he's stepped
Into a great estate. When he was poor,
Imprisoned, and in scarcity of friends,
I cleared him with five talents. Greet him from me,
Bid him suppose good necessity
Touches his friend, which craves to be rememb'red
With those five talents. That had, give't these fellows

To whom 'tis instant due. Nev'r speak or think
That Timon's fortunes 'mong his friends can sink.

Flavius. I would I could not think it; that thought is bounty's foe.
Being free itself, it thinks all others so.

[*Exeunt*]

ACT THREE

LUCULLUS' HOUSE

[Flaminius waiting to speak with Lord Lucul-
lus from his Master, enters a Servant to him]

Servant.   I have told my lord of you; he is coming down to you.

Flaminius.   I thank you, sir.

         [Enter Lucullus]

Servant.   Here's my lord.

Lucullus.   *[Aside]* One of Lord Timon's men? A gift I warrant. Why this hits right; I dreamt of a silver basin and ewer tonight.—Flaminius, honest Flaminius, you are very respectively welcome, sir. Fill me some wine. *[Exit Servant]* And how does that honorable, complete, free-hearted gentleman of Athens, thy very bountiful good lord and master?

Flaminius.   His health is well, sir.

Lucullus.   I am right glad that his health is well, sir. And what hast thou there under thy cloak, pretty Flaminius?

Flaminius.   Faith, nothing but an empty box, sir, which in my lord's behalf I come to entreat your honor to supply;

who, having great and instant occasion to use fifty talents, hath sent to your lordship to furnish him, nothing doubting your present assistance therein.

Lucullus. La, la, la, la! "Nothing doubting," says he? Alas, good lord, a noble gentleman 'tis, if he would not keep so good a house. Many a time and often I ha' dined with him, and told him on't, and come again to supper to him of purpose to have him spend less, and yet he would embrace no counsel, take no warning by my coming. Every man has his fault, and honesty is his. I ha' told him on't, but I could ne'er get him from't.

[*Enter Servant, with wine*]

Servant. Please your lordship, here is the wine.

Lucullus. Flaminius, I have noted thee always wise. Here's to thee.

Flaminius. Your lordship speaks your pleasure.

Lucullus. I have observed thee always for a towardly prompt spirit, give thee thy due, and one that knows what belongs to reason; and canst use the time well, if the

time use thee well. Good parts in thee. [*To Servant*]
Get you gone, sirrah. [*Exit Servant*] Draw nearer,
honest Flaminius. Thy lord's a bountiful gentleman,
but thou art wise, and thou know'st well enough,
although thou com'st to me, that this is no time to
lend money, especially upon bare friendship without
security. Here's three solidares for thee. Good boy,
wink at me, and say thou saw'st me not. Fare thee
well.

Flaminius.   Is't possible the world should so much differ,
And we alive that lived? Fly, damnèd baseness,
To him that worships thee.
       [*Throws back the money*]

Lucullus.   Ha? Now I see thou art a fool, and fit for thy master.
       [*Exit*]

Flaminius.   May these add to the number that may scald thee.
Let molten coin be thy damnation,
Thou disease of a friend, and not himself.
Has friendship such a faint and milky heart
It turns in less than two nights? O you gods!

I feel my master's passion. This slave
Unto his honor has my lord's meat in him;
Why should it thrive and turn to nutriment
When he is turned to poison?
O may diseases only work upon't,
And when he's sick to death, let not that part of nature
Which my lord paid for be of any power
To expel sickness, but prolong his hour.
    [Exit]

A PUBLIC PLACE

[Enter Lucius, with three Strangers]

Lucius.   Who, the Lord Timon? He is my very good friend and an honorable gentleman.

First Stranger.   We know him for no less, though we are but strangers to him. But I can tell you one thing, my lord, and which I hear from common rumors: now Lord Timon's happy hours are done and past, and his estate shrinks from him.

Lucius.   Fie, no, do not believe it; he cannot want for money.

Second Stranger.   But believe you this, my lord, that not long ago, one of his men was with the Lord Lucullus to borrow so many talents, nay urged extremely for't, and showed what necessity belonged to't, and yet was denied.

Lucius.   How?

Second Stranger.   I tell you, denied, my lord.

Lucius.   What a strange case was that! Now before the gods I am ashamed on't. Denied that honorable man? There was very little honor showed in't. For my

own part, I must needs confess, I have received
some small kindnesses from him, as money, plate,
jewels, and suchlike trifles, nothing comparing to
his; yet had he mistook him and sent to me, I should
ne'er have denied his occasion so many talents.

      [Enter Servilius]

Servilius. See, by good hap, yonder's my lord; I have sweat to
see his honor. My honored lord.

Lucius. Servilius? You are kindly met, sir. Fare thee well;
commend me to thy honorable virtuous lord, my
very exquisite friend.

Servilius. May it please your honor, my lord hath sent —

Lucius. Ha? What has he sent? I am so much endeared to
that lord; he's ever sending. How shall I thank him,
think'st thou? And what has he sent now?

Servilius. Has only sent his present occasion now, my lord,
requesting your lordship to supply his instant use
with so many talents.

Lucius. I know his lordship is but merry with me,
He cannot want fifty-five-hundred talents.

Servilius. But in the meantime he wants less, my lord.
If his occasion were not virtuous,
I should not urge it half so faithfully.

Lucius. Dost thou speak seriously, Servilius?

Servilius. Upon my soul 'tis true, sir.

Lucius. What a wicked beast was I to disfurnish myself against such a good time, when I might ha' shown myself honorable! How unluckily it happ'ned that I should purchase the day before for a little part, and undo a great deal of honor! Servilius, now before the gods I am not able to do—the more beast, I say! I was sending to use Lord Timon myself, these gentlemen can witness; but I would not for the wealth of Athens I had done't now. Commend me bountifully to his good lordship, and I hope his honor will conceive the fairest of me, because I have no power to be kind. And tell him this from me, I count it one of my greatest afflictions, say, that I cannot pleasure such an honorable gentleman. Good Servilius, will you befriend me so far as to use mine own words to him?

Servilius.	Yes, sir, I shall.
Lucius.	I'll look you out a good turn, Servilius.

        [*Exit Servilius*]

True, as you said, Timon is shrunk indeed,
And he that's once denied will hardly speed.

        [*Exit*]

First Stranger.	Do you observe this, Hostilius?
Second Stranger.	Ay, too well.
First Stranger.	Why this is the world's soul, and just of the same piece

Is every flatterer's sport. Who can call him his friend
That dips in the same dish? For in my knowing
Timon has been this lord's father,
And kept his credit with his purse;
Supported his estate; nay, Timon's money
Has paid his men their wages. He ne'er drinks
But Timon's silver treads upon his lip,
And yet—O see the monstrousness of man
When he looks out in an ungrateful shape—
He does deny him, in respect of his,
What charitable men afford to beggars.

Third Stranger.   Religion groans at it.

First Stranger.   For mine own part,
I never tasted Timon in my life,
Nor came any of his bounties over me
To mark me for his friend. Yet I protest,
For his right noble mind, illustrious virtue,
And honorable carriage,
Had his necessity made use of me,
I would have put my wealth into donation,
And the best half should have returned to him,
So much I love his heart. But I perceive
Men must learn now with pity to dispense,
For policy sits above conscience.

    [Exeunt]

SEMPRONIUS' HOUSE

[*Enter a Third Servant of Timon with*
Sempronius, another of Timon's friends]

Sempronius. Must he needs trouble me in't—humh!—'bove all others?
He might have tried Lord Lucius or Lucullus,
And now Ventidius is wealthy too,
Whom he redeemed from prison. All these
Owes their estates unto him.

Third Servant.   My lord,
They have all been touched and found base metal,
For they have all denied him.

Sempronius.   How? Have they denied him?
Has Ventidius and Lucullus denied him,
And does he send to me? Three? Humh!
It shows but little love or judgment in him.
Must I be his last refuge? His friends, like physicians,
Thrive, give him over. Must I take th' cure upon me?
Has much disgraced me in't; I'm angry at him
That might have known my place. I see no sense for't,

But his occasions might have wooed me first;
For, in my conscience, I was the first man
That e'er received gift from him.
And does he think so backwardly of me now
That I'll requite it last? No.
So it may prove an argument of laughter
To th' rest, and I 'mongst lords be thought a fool.
I'd rather than the worth of thrice the sum,
Had sent to me first, but for my mind's sake;
I'd such a courage to do him good. But now return,
And with their faint reply this answer join:
Who bates mine honor shall not know my coin.
      [Exit]

Third Servant. Excellent. Your lordship's a goodly villain. The
devil knew not what he did when he made man
politic; he crossed himself by't: and I cannot think
but in the end the villainies of man will set him clear.
How fairly this lord strives to appear foul! Takes
virtuous copies to be wicked. Like those that under
hot ardent zeal would set whole realms on fire, of

such a nature is his politic love.
This was my lord's best hope; now all are fled
Save only the gods. Now his friends are dead,
Doors that were ne'er acquainted with their wards
Many a bounteous year, must be employed
Now to guard sure their master.
And this is all a liberal course allows;
Who cannot keep his wealth must keep his house.

　　　[*Exit*]

TIMON'S HOUSE

[*Enter Varro's two Servants, meeting others.*
All the Servants of Timon's creditors wait
for his coming out. Then enter the servant
of Lucius; then Titus and Hortensius]

Varro's First Servant. Well met; good morrow, Titus and Hortensius.

Titus. The like to you, kind Varro.

Hortensius.   Lucius!
What, do we meet together?

Lucius' Servant.   Ay, and I think
One business does command us all;
For mine is money.

Titus.   So is theirs and ours.

      [*Enter Philotus*]

Lucius' Servant. And, sir, Philotus' too!

Philotus.   Good day at once.

Lucius' Servant. Welcome, good brother. What do you think the hour?

Philotus. Laboring for nine.

Lucius' Servant. So much?

Philotus.	Is not my lord seen yet?
Lucius' Servant.	Not yet.
Philotus.	I wonder on't; he was wont to shine at seven.
Lucius' Servant.	Ay, but the days are waxed shorter with him.
	You must consider that a prodigal course
	Is like the sun's,
	But not like his recoverable, I fear.
	'Tis deepest winter in Lord Timon's purse;
	That is, one may reach deep enough and yet
	Find little.
Philotus.	I am of your fear for that.
Titus.	I'll show you how t' observe a strange event.
	Your lord sends now for money?
Hortensius.	Most true, he does.
Titus.	And he wears jewels now of Timon's gift,
	For which I wait for money.
Hortensius.	It is against my heart.
Lucius' Servant.	Mark how strange it shows,
	Timon in this should pay more than he owes;
	And e'en as if your lord should wear rich jewels

And send for money for 'em.

Hortensius. I'm weary of this charge, the gods can witness.
I know my lord hath spent of Timon's wealth,
And now ingratitude makes it worse than stealth.

Varro's First Servant. Yes, mine's three thousand crowns. What's yours?

Lucius' Servant. Five thousand mine.

Varro's First Servant. 'Tis much deep, and it should seem by th' sum
Your master's confidence was above mine,
Else surely his had equaled.

        [*Enter Flaminius*]

Titus. One of Lord Timon's men.

Lucius' Servant. Flaminius? Sir, a word. Pray is my lord ready to
come forth?

Flaminius. No, indeed he is not.

Titus. We attend his lordship; pray signify so much.

Flaminius. I need not tell him that; he knows you are too diligent.

        [*Exit*]

        [*Enter Flavius, the Steward, in a cloak, muffled*]

Lucius' Servant. Ha! Is not that his steward muffled so?
He goes away in a cloud. Call him, call him.

Titus. Do you hear, sir?

Varro's Second Servant. By your leave, sir.

Flavius. What do ye ask of me, my friend?

Titus. We wait for certain money here, sir.

Flavius.   Ay,

If money were as certain as your waiting,

'Twere sure enough.

Why then preferred you not your sums and bills

When your false masters ate of my lord's meat?

Then they could smile, and fawn upon his debts,

And take down th' int'rest into their glutt'nous maws.

You do yourselves but wrong to stir me up;

Let me pass quietly.

Believe't, my lord and I have made an end;

I have no more to reckon, he to spend.

Lucius' Servant. Ay, but this answer will not serve.

Flavius. If 'twill not serve, 'tis not so base as you,

For you serve knaves.

           {*Exit*}

Varro's First Servant. How? What does his cashiered worship mutter?

Varro's Second Servant. No matter what; he's poor, and that's revenge enough. Who can speak broader than he that has no house to put his head in? Such may rail against great buildings.

                    [*Enter Servilius*]

Titus. O here's Servilius. Now we shall know some answer.

Servilius. If I might beseech you, gentlemen, to repair some other hour, I should derive much from't. For take't of my soul, my lord leans wondrously to discontent. His comfortable temper has forsook him, he's much out of health, and keeps his chamber.

Lucius' Servant. Many do keep their chambers are not sick;
And if it be so far beyond his health,
Methinks he should the sooner pay his debts,
And make a clear way to the gods.

Servilius.   Good gods!

Titus. We cannot take this for answer, sir.

Flaminius. [*Within*] Servilius, help! My lord, my lord!

                    [*Enter Timon in a rage*]

Timon. What, are my doors opposed against my passage?

Have I been ever free, and must my house
Be my retentive enemy? My jail?
The place which I have feasted, does it now,
Like all mankind, show me an iron heart?

Lucius' Servant. Put in now, Titus.

Titus. My lord, here is my bill.

Lucius' Servant. Here's mine.

Hortensius. And mine, my lord.

Both Varro's Servants. And ours, my lord.

Philotus. All our bills.

Timon. Knock me down with 'em, cleave me to the girdle.

Lucius' Servant. Alas, my lord —

Timon. Cut my heart in sums.

Titus. Mine, fifty talents.

Timon. Tell out my blood.

Lucius' Servant. Five thousand crowns, my lord.

Timon. Five thousand drops pays that. What yours? And yours?

Varro's First Servant. My lord —

Varro's Second Servant. My lord —

Timon. Tear me, take me, and the gods fall upon you.

[Exit Timon]

Hortensius. Faith, I perceive our masters may throw their caps
at their money; these debts may well be called
desperate ones, for a madman owes 'em.

[Exeunt]

[Enter Timon and Flavius]

Timon. They have e'en put my breath from me, the slaves.
Creditors? Devils!

Flavius My dear lord—

Timon. What if it should be so?

Flavius. My lord—

Timon. I'll have it so. My steward!

Flavius. Here, my lord.

Timon. So fitly? Go, bid all my friends again,
Lucius, Lucullus, and Sempronius—all.
I'll once more feast the rascals.

Flavius.   O my lord,
You only speak from your distracted soul;
There's not so much left to furnish out
A moderate table.

Timon. Be it not in thy care.
Go, I charge thee, invite them all, let in the tide
Of knaves once more; my cook and I'll provide.
[*Exeunt*]

THE SENATE HOUSE

[*Enter three Senators all at one door,*
Alcibiades meeting them with Attendants]

First Senator.   My lord, you have my voice to't. The fault's
Bloody; 'tis necessary he should die.
Nothing emboldens sin so much as mercy.

Second Senator.   Most true; the law shall bruise 'em.

Alcibiades.   Honor, health, and compassion to the senate.

First Senator.   Now, captain?

Alcibiades.   I am an humble suitor to your virtues;
For pity is the virtue of the law,
And none but tyrants use it cruelly.
It pleases time and fortune to lie heavy
Upon a friend of mine, who in hot blood
Hath stepped into the law; which is past depth
To those that, without heed, do plunge into't.
He is a man, setting his fate aside,
Of comely virtues;
Nor did he soil the fact with cowardice

(An honor in him which buys out his fault),
But with a noble fury and fair spirit,
Seeing his reputation touched to death,
He did oppose his foe;
And with such sober and unnoted passion
He did behove his anger, ere 'twas spent,
As if he had but proved an argument.

First Senator. You undergo too strict a paradox,
Striving to make an ugly deed look fair.
Your words have took such pains as if they labored
To bring manslaughter into form, and set
Quarreling upon the head of valor, which indeed
Is valor misbegot, and came into the world
When sects and factions were newly born.
He's truly valiant that can wisely suffer
The worst that man can breathe,
And make his wrongs his outsides,
To wear them like his raiment, carelessly,
And ne'er prefer his injuries to his heart,
To bring it into danger.

If wrongs be evils and enforce us kill,
What folly 'tis to hazard life for ill.

Alcibiades.   My lord—

First Senator.   You cannot make gross sins look clear.
To revenge is no valor, but to bear.

Alcibiades.   My lords, then, under favor, pardon me,
If I speak like a captain.
Why do fond men expose themselves to battle,
And not endure all threats? Sleep upon't,
And let the foes quietly cut their throats
Without repugnancy? If there be
Such valor in the bearing, what make we
Abroad? Why then, women are more valiant
That stay at home, if bearing carry it,
And the ass more captain than the lion, the fellow
Loaden with irons wiser than the judge,
If wisdom be in suffering. O my lords,
As you are great, be pitifully good.
Who cannot condemn rashness in cold blood?
To kill, I grant, is sin's extremest gust,

But in defense, by mercy, 'tis most just.
To be in anger is impiety;
But who is man that is not angry?
Weigh but the crime with this.

Second Senator. You breathe in vain.

Alcibiades.   In vain? His service done
At Lacedaemon and Byzantium
Were a sufficient briber for his life.

First Senator. What's that?

Alcibiades.   Why say, my lords, h'as done fair service,
And slain in fight many of your enemies.
How full of valor did he bear himself
In the last conflict, and made plenteous wounds!

Second Senator. He has made too much plenty with 'em.
He's a sworn rioter; he has a sin that often
Drowns him and takes his valor prisoner.
If there were no foes, that were enough
To overcome him. In that beastly fury
He has been known to commit outrages,
And cherish factions. 'Tis inferred to us

                  His days are foul and his drink dangerous.

First Senator.   He dies.

Alcibiades.   Hard fate. He might have died in war.
My lords, if not for any parts in him —
Though his right arm might purchase his own time,
And be in debt to none — yet, more to move you,
Take my deserts to his, and join 'em both.
And for I know your reverend ages love
Security, I'll pawn my victories, all
My honor to you, upon his good returns.
If by this crime he owes the law his life,
Why, let the war receiv't in valiant gore,
For law is strict, and war is nothing more.

First Senator.   We are for law. He dies. Urge it no more,
On height of our displeasure. Friend or brother,
He forfeits his own blood that spills another.

Alcibiades.   Must it be so? It must not be.
My lords, I do beseech you know me.

Second Senator.   How?

Alcibiades.   Call me to your remembrances.

Third Senator.   What?

Alcibiades.   I cannot think but your age has forgot me;
It could not else be I should prove so base
To sue and be denied such common grace.
My wounds ache at you.

First Senator.   Do you dare our anger?
'Tis in few words, but spacious in effect:
We banish thee for ever.

Alcibiades.   Banish me?
Banish your dotage, banish usury,
That makes the senate ugly.

First Senator.   If after two days' shine Athens contain thee,
Attend our weightier judgment. And, not to swell our spirit,
He shall be executed presently.

        {Exeunt Senators}

Alcibiades.   Now the gods keep you old enough, that you may live
Only in bone, that none may look on you.
I'm worse than mad. I have kept back their foes,
While they have told their money, and let out
Their coin upon large interest, I myself

Rich only in large hurts. All those, for this?
Is this the balsam that the usuring Senate
Pours into captains' wounds? Banishment!
It comes not ill. I hate not to be banished;
It is a cause worthy my spleen and fury,
That I may strike at Athens. I'll cheer up
My discontented troops and lay for hearts.
'Tis honor with most lands to be at odds;
Soldiers should brook as little wrongs as gods.
    [*Exit*]

A BANQUETING HALL IN TIMON'S HOUSE

[*Music. Tables set out, Servants attending.*
Enter divers Friends of Timon at several doors]

First Lord. The good time of day to you, sir.

Second Lord. I also wish it to you. I think this honorable lord did but try us this other day.

First Lord. Upon that were my thoughts tiring when we encount'red. I hope it is not so low with him as he made it seem in the trial of his several friends.

Second Lord. It should not be, by the persuasion of his new feasting.

First Lord. I should think so. He hath sent me an earnest inviting, which many my near occasions did urge me to put off; but he hath conjured me beyond them, and I must needs appear.

Second Lord. In like manner was I in debt to my importunate business, but he would not hear my excuse. I am sorry, when he sent to borrow of me, that my provision was out.

First Lord.   I am sick of that grief too, as I understand how all things go.

Second Lord.   Every man here's so. What would he have borrowed of you?

First Lord.   A thousand pieces.

Second Lord.   A thousand pieces?

First Lord.   What of you?

Second Lord.   He sent to me, sir—

          [*Enter Timon and Attendants*]

                    Here he comes.

Timon.   With all my heart, gentlemen both; and how fare you?

First Lord.   Ever at the best, hearing well of your lordship.

Second Lord.   The swallow follows not summer more willing than we your lordship.

Timon.   [*Aside*] Nor more willingly leaves winter, such summer birds are men.—Gentlemen, our dinner will not recompense this long stay. Feast your ears with the music awhile, if they will fare so harshly o' th' trumpet's sound; we shall to't presently.

First Lord. I hope it remains not unkindly with your lordship
that I returned you an empty messenger.

Timon. O sir, let it not trouble you.

Second Lord. My noble lord —

Timon. Ah my good friend, what cheer?

Second Lord. My most honorable lord, I am e'en sick of shame
that when your lordship this other day sent to me, I
was so unfortunate a beggar.

Timon. Think not on't, sir.

Second Lord. If you had sent but two hours before —

Timon. Let it not cumber your better remembrance.

   [*The banquet brought in*]

Come, bring in all together.

Second Lord. All covered dishes.

First Lord. Royal cheer, I warrant you.

Third Lord. Doubt not that, if money and the season can yield it.

First Lord. How do you? What's the news?

Third Lord. Alcibiades is banished. Hear you of it?

First and Second Lords. Alcibiades banished?

Third Lord. 'Tis so, be sure of it.

First Lord.   How? How?

Second Lord.   I pray you upon what?

Timon.   My worthy friends, will you draw near?

Third Lord.   I'll tell you more anon. Here's a noble feast toward.

Second Lord.   This is the old man still.

Third Lord.   Will't hold? Will't hold?

Second Lord.   It does; but time will—and so—

Third Lord.   I do conceive.

Timon.   Each man to his stool, with that spur as he would to the lip of his mistress. Your diet shall be in all places alike. Make not a city feast of it, to let the meat cool ere we can agree upon the first place. Sit, sit. The gods require our thanks.

You great benefactors, sprinkle our society with thankfulness. For your own gifts, make yourselves praised. But reserve still to give, lest your deities be despised. Lend to each man enough that one need not lend to another; for were your godheads to borrow of men, men would forsake the gods. Make the meat be beloved more than the man that gives it.

Let no assembly of twenty be without a score of villains. If there sit twelve women at the table, let a dozen of them be as they are. The rest of your fees, O gods — the senators of Athens, together with the common leg of people — what is amiss in them, you gods, make suitable for destruction. For these my present friends, as they are to me nothing, so in nothing bless them, and to nothing are they welcome.

Uncover, dogs, and lap.

    [*The dishes are uncovered and seen to be full of water*]

Some speak.	What does his lordship mean?
Some other.	I know not.
Timon.	May you a better feast never behold,

You knot of mouth-friends. Smoke and lukewarm water
Is your perfection. This is Timon's last,
Who, stuck and spangled with your flatteries,
Washes it off and sprinkles in your faces
Your reeking villainy.

    [*Throws the water in their faces*]

       Live loathed and long,
Most smiling, smooth, detested parasites,
Courteous destroyers, affable wolves, meek bears,
You fools of fortune, trencher-friends, time's flies,
Cap-and-knee slaves, vapors, and minute-jacks.
Of man and beast the infinite malady
Crust you quite o'er. What, dost thou go?
Soft, take thy physic first; thou too, and thou.
Stay, I will lend thee money, borrow none.
   [*Drives them out*]
What? All in motion? Henceforth be no feast,
Whereat a villain's not a welcome guest.
Burn house, sink Athens, henceforth hated be
Of Timon man and all humanity.
   [*Exit*]
   [*Enter the Senators, with other Lords*]

First Lord. How now, my lords?
Second Lord. Know you the quality of Lord Timon's fury?
Third Lord. Push, did you see my cap?
Fourth Lord. I have lost my gown.

First Lord.   He's but a mad lord, and naught but humors sways
him. He gave me a jewel th' other day, and now he
has beat it out of my hat. Did you see my jewel?

Third Lord.   Did you see my cap?

Second Lord.   Here 'tis.

Fourth Lord.   Here lies my gown.

First Lord.   Let's make no stay.

Second Lord.   Lord Timon's mad.

Third Lord.   I feel't upon my bones.

Fourth Lord.   One day he gives us diamonds, next day stones.

            [*Exeunt the Senators and others*]

ACT FOUR

OUTSIDE THE WALLS OF ATHENS

[Enter Timon]

Timon. Let me look back upon thee. O thou wall
That girdles in those wolves, dive in the earth,
And fence not Athens. Matrons, turn incontinent;
Obedience fail in children. Slaves and fools,
Pluck the grave wrinkled senate from the bench,
And minister in their steads. To general filths
Convert o' th' instant green virginity;
Do't in your parents' eyes. Bankrupts, hold fast
Rather than render back; out with your knives,
And cut your trusters' throats. Bound servants, steal;
Large-handed robbers your grave masters are,
And pill by law. Maid, to thy master's bed,
Thy mistress is o' th' brothel. Son of sixteen,
Pluck the lined crutch from thy old limping sire,
With it beat out his brains. Piety, and fear,
Religion to the gods, peace, justice, truth,
Domestic awe, night-rest, and neighborhood,

Instruction, manners, mysteries, and trades,
Degrees, observances, customs, and laws,
Decline to your confounding contraries,
And let confusion live. Plagues incident to men,
Your potent and infectious fevers heap
On Athens ripe for stroke. Thou cold sciatica,
Cripple our senators, that their limbs may halt
As lamely as their manners. Lust and liberty
Creep in the minds and marrows of our youth,
That 'gainst the stream of virtue they may strive,
And drown themselves in riot. Itches, blains,
Sow all th' Athenian bosoms, and their crop
Be general leprosy. Breath infect breath,
That their society, as their friendship, may
Be merely poison. Nothing I'll bear from thee
But nakedness, thou detestable town;
Take thou that too, with multiplying bans.
Timon will to the woods, where he shall find
Th' unkindest beast more kinder than mankind.
The gods confound—hear me, you good gods all—

Th' Athenians both within and out that wall.
And grant, as Timon grows, his hate may grow
To the whole race of mankind, high and low.
Amen.

    [Exit]

ATHENS. TIMON'S HOUSE

[Enter Flavius, the Steward, with two or three Servants]

First Servant. Hear you, master steward, where's our master?
Are we undone, cast off, nothing remaining?

Flavius. Alack, my fellows, what should I say to you?
Let me be recorded by the righteous gods,
I am as poor as you.

First Servant.   Such a house broke?
So noble a master fall'n, all gone, and not
One friend to take his fortune by the arm,
And go along with him?

Second Servant.   As we do turn our backs
From our companion thrown into his grave,
So his familiars to his buried fortunes
Slink all away, leave their false vows with him,
Like empty purses picked; and his poor self,
A dedicated beggar to the air,
With his disease of all-shunned poverty,
Walks like contempt alone.

[*Enter other Servants*]

                                        More of our fellows.

Flavius.   All broken implements of a ruined house.

Third Servant.   Yet do our hearts wear Timon's livery,
                   That see I by our faces; we are fellows still,
                   Serving alike in sorrow. Leaked is our bark,
                   And we poor mates stand on the dying deck,
                   Hearing the surges threat. We must all part
                   Into this sea of air.

Flavius.   Good fellows all,
                   The latest of my wealth I'll share amongst you.
                   Wherever we shall meet, for Timon's sake,
                   Let's yet be fellows. Let's shake our heads and say,
                   As 'twere a knell unto our master's fortunes,
                   "We have seen better days." Let each take some.
                        [*Gives money*]
                   Nay, put out all your hands. Not one word more;
                   Thus part we rich in sorrow, parting poor.
                        [*Embrace, and part several ways*]
                   O the fierce wretchedness that glory brings us!

Who would not wish to be from wealth exempt,
Since riches point to misery and contempt?
Who would be so mocked with glory, or to live
But in a dream of friendship,
To have his pomp and all what state compounds
But only painted, like his varnished friends?
Poor honest lord, brought low by his own heart,
Undone by goodness. Strange, unusual blood,
When man's worst sin is, he does too much good.
Who then dares to be half so kind again?
For bounty, that makes gods, do still mar men.
My dearest lord, blessed to be most accursed,
Rich only to be wretched, thy great fortunes
Are made thy chief afflictions. Alas, kind lord,
He's flung in rage from this ingrateful seat
Of monstrous friends;
Nor has he with him to supply his life,
Or that which can command it.
I'll follow and inquire him out.
I'll ever serve his mind with my best will;

Whilst I have gold, I'll be his steward still.
[Exit]

BEFORE TIMON'S CAVE

[Enter Timon in the woods]

Timon.   O blessèd breeding sun, draw from the earth
Rotten humidity; below thy sister's orb
Infect the air. Twinned brothers of one womb,
Whose procreation, residence, and birth,
Scarce is dividant—touch them with several fortunes,
The greater scorns the lesser. Not nature,
To whom all sores lay siege, can bear great fortune
But by contempt of nature.
Raise me this beggar, and deny't that lord,
The senators shall bear contempt hereditary,
The beggar native honor.
It is the pasture lards the brother's sides,
The want that makes him lean. Who dares? Who dares
In purity of manhood stand upright
And say, this man's a flatterer? If one be,
So are they all, for every grise of fortune
Is smoothed by that below. The learned pate

Ducks to the golden fool. All's obliquy;
There's nothing level in our cursèd natures
But direct villainy. Therefore be abhorred
All feasts, societies, and throngs of men.
His semblable, yea himself, Timon disdains;
Destruction fang mankind. Earth, yield me roots.
     [Digs]
Who seeks for better of thee, sauce his palate
With thy most operant poison. What is here?
Gold? Yellow, glittering, precious gold?
No, gods, I am no idle votarist.
Roots, you clear heavens! Thus much of this will make
Black, white; foul, fair; wrong, right;
Base, noble; old, young; coward, valiant.
Ha, you gods! Why this? What this, you gods? Why this
Will lug your priests and servants from your sides;
Pluck stout men's pillows from below their heads.
This yellow slave
Will knit and break religions, bless th' accursed,
Make the hoar leprosy adored, place thieves,

And give them title, knee, and approbation
With senators on the bench. This is it
That makes the wappened widow wed again;
She, whom the spital-house and ulcerous sores
Would cast the gorge at, this embalms and spices
To th' April day again. Come, damned earth,
Thou common whore of mankind, that puts odds
Among the rout of nations, I will make thee
Do thy right nature.
        [*March afar off*]

                            Ha? A drum? Th'art quick,
But yet I'll bury thee. Thou't go, strong thief,
When gouty keepers of thee cannot stand.
Nay, stay thou out for earnest.
        [*Keeps some gold*]
        [*Enter Alcibiades, with drum and fife, in
            warlike manner; and Phrynia and Timandra*]

Alcibiades. What art thou there? Speak.
Timon.   A beast as thou art. The canker gnaw thy heart
For showing me again the eyes of man.

Alcibiades.	What is thy name? Is man so hateful to thee
	That art thyself a man?
Timon.	I am Misanthropos and hate mankind.
	For thy part, I do wish thou wert a dog,
	That I might love thee something.
Alcibiades.	I know thee well,
	But in thy fortunes am unlearned and strange.
Timon.	I know thee too, and more than that I know thee
	I not desire to know. Follow thy drum,
	With man's blood paint the ground gules, gules.
	Religious canons, civil laws are cruel;
	Then what should war be? This fell whore of thine
	Hath in her more destruction than thy sword,
	For all her cherubin look.
Phrynia.	Thy lips rot off.
Timon.	I will not kiss thee; then the rot returns
	To thine own lips again.
Alcibiades.	How came the noble Timon to this change?
Timon.	As the moon does, by wanting light to give.
	But then renew I could not like the moon;

There were no suns to borrow of.

Alcibiades.   Noble Timon, what friendship may I do thee?

Timon.   None, but to maintain my opinion.

Alcibiades.   What is it, Timon?

Timon.   Promise me friendship, but perform none.
If thou wilt not promise, the gods plague thee,
For thou art a man. If thou dost perform,
Confound thee, for thou art a man.

Alcibiades.   I have heard in some sort of thy miseries.

Timon.   Thou saw'st them when I had prosperity.

Alcibiades.   I see them now; then was a blessed time.

Timon.   As thine is now, held with a brace of harlots.

Timandra.   Is this th' Athenian minion, whom the world
Voiced so regardfully?

Timon.   Art thou Timandra?

Timandra.   Yes.

Timon.   Be a whore still; they love thee not that use thee.
Give them diseases, leaving with thee their lust.
Make use of thy salt hours. Season the slaves
For tubs and baths; bring down rose-cheeked youth

	To the tub-fast and the diet.
Timandra.	Hang thee, monster!
Alcibiades.	Pardon him, sweet Timandra, for his wits
	Are drowned and lost in his calamities.
	I have but little gold of late, brave Timon,
	The want whereof doth daily make revolt
	In my penurious band. I have heard, and grieved,
	How cursèd Athens, mindless of thy worth,
	Forgetting thy great deeds, when neighbor states,
	But for thy sword and fortune, trod upon them—
Timon.	I prithee beat thy drum and get thee gone.
Alcibiades.	I am thy friend and pity thee, dear Timon.
Timon.	How dost thou pity him whom thou dost trouble?
	I had rather be alone.
Alcibiades.	Why fare thee well.
	Here is some gold for thee.
Timon.	Keep it, I cannot eat it.
Alcibiades.	When I have laid proud Athens on a heap—
Timon.	War'st thou 'gainst Athens?
Alcibiades.	Ay, Timon, and have cause.

Timon.   The gods confound them all in thy conquest,
And thee after when thou hast conquerèd.

Alcibiades.   Why me, Timon?

Timon.   That by killing of villains
Thou wast born to conquer my country.
Put up thy gold. Go on, here's gold, go on.
Be as a planetary plague, when Jove
Will o'er some high-viced city hang his poison
In the sick air. Let not thy sword skip one.
Pity not honored age for his white beard:
He is an usurer. Strike me the counterfeit matron:
It is her habit only that is honest,
Herself's a bawd. Let not the virgin's cheek
Make soft thy trenchant sword: for those milk paps,
That through the window-bars bore at men's eyes,
Are not within the leaf of pity writ,
But set them down horrible traitors. Spare not the babe
Whose dimpled smiles from fools exhaust their mercy:
Think it a bastard, whom the oracle
Hath doubtfully pronounced thy throat shall cut,

And mince it sans remorse. Swear against objects.
Put armor on thine ears and on thine eyes,
Whose proof nor yells of mothers, maids, nor babes,
Nor sight of priests in holy vestments bleeding,
Shall pierce a jot. There's gold to pay thy soldiers.
Make large confusion; and, thy fury spent,
Confounded be thyself. Speak not, begone.

Alcibiades. Hast thou gold yet, I'll take the gold thou givest me,
Not all thy counsel.

Timon. Dost thou or dost thou not, heaven's curse upon thee.

Phrynia and Timandra. Give us some gold, good Timon; hast thou more?

Timon. Enough to make a whore forswear her trade,
And to make whores, a bawd. Hold up, you sluts,
Your aprons mountant. You are not oathable,
Although I know you'll swear, terribly swear
Into strong shudders and to heavenly agues
Th' immortal gods that hear you. Spare your oaths;
I'll trust to your conditions. Be whores still,
And he whose pious breath seeks to convert you,
Be strong in whore, allure him, burn him up;

Let your close fire predominate his smoke,
And be no turncoats. Yet may your pains six months
Be quite contrary. And thatch
Your poor thin roofs with burdens of the dead—
Some that were hanged, no matter.
Wear them, betray with them; whore still;
Paint till a horse may mire upon your face.
A pox of wrinkles!

Phrynia and Timandra. Well, more gold. What then?
Believ't that we'll do anything for gold.

Timon. Consumptions sow
In hollow bones of man; strike their sharp shins,
And mar men's spurring. Crack the lawyer's voice,
That he may never more false title plead,
Nor sound his quillets shrilly. Hoar the flamen,
That scolds against the quality of flesh
And not believes himself. Down with the nose,
Down with it flat, take the bridge quite away
Of him, that his particular to foresee,
Smells from the general weal. Make curled-pate ruffians bald,

And let the unscarred braggarts of the war
Derive some pain from you. Plague all,
That your activity may defeat and quell
The source of all erection. There's more gold.
Do you damn others, and let this damn you,
And ditches grave you all.

Phrynia and Timandra. More counsel with more money, bounteous Timon.

Timon. More whore, more mischief first; I have given you earnest.

Alcibiades. Strike up the drum towards Athens. Farewell, Timon.
If I thrive well, I'll visit thee again.

Timon. If I hope well, I'll never see thee more.

Alcibiades. I never did thee harm.

Timon. Yes, thou spok'st well of me.

Alcibiades.   Call'st thou that harm?

Timon. Men daily find it. Get thee away, and take
Thy beagles with thee.

Alcibiades.   We but offend him. Strike!

[Drum beats. Exeunt Alcibiades, Phrynia, and Timandra]

Timon. That nature, being sick of man's unkindness,
Should yet be hungry! Common mother, thou,
          [Digging]

Whose womb unmeasurable and infinite breast
Teems and feeds all; whose selfsame mettle,
Whereof thy proud child, arrogant man, is puffed,
Engenders the black toad and adder blue,
The gilded newt and eyeless venomed worm,
With all th' abhorrèd births below crisp heaven
Whereon Hyperion's quick'ning fire doth shine;
Yield him, who all the human sons do hate,
From forth thy plenteous bosom, one poor root.
Ensear thy fertile and conceptious womb;
Let it no more bring out ingrateful man.
Go great with tigers, dragons, wolves, and bears,
Teem with new monsters, whom thy upward face
Hath to the marbled mansion all above
Never presented. O, a root, dear thanks!
Dry up thy marrows, vines and plough-torn leas,
Whereof ingrateful man, with liquorish draughts
And morsels unctious, greases his pure mind,
That from it all consideration slips —

　　[*Enter Apemantus*]

More man? Plague, plague!

Apemantus.   I was directed hither. Men report
Thou dost affect my manners, and dost use them.

Timon.   'Tis then because thou dost not keep a dog
Whom I would imitate. Consumption catch thee.

Apemantus.   This is in thee a nature but infected,
A poor unmanly melancholy sprung
From change of future. Why this spade? This place?
This slave-like habit and these looks of care?
Thy flatterers yet wear silk, drink wine, lie soft,
Hug their diseased perfumes, and have forgot
That ever Timon was. Shame not these woods
By putting on the cunning of a carper.
Be thou a flatterer now, and seek to thrive
By that which has undone thee. Hinge thy knee,
And let his very breath whom thou'lt observe
Blow off thy cap; praise his most vicious strain
And call it excellent. Thou wast told thus.
Thou gav'st thine ears, like tapsters that bade welcome,
To knaves and all approachers. 'Tis most just

That thou turn rascal; hadst thou wealth again,

Rascals should have't. Do not assume my likeness.

Timon.   Were I like thee, I'd throw away myself.

Apemantus.   Thou hast cast away thyself, being like thyself:

A madman so long, now a fool. What, think'st

That the bleak air, thy boisterous chamberlain,

Will put thy shirt on warm? Will these moist trees,

That have outlived the eagle, page thy heels

And skip when thou point'st out? Will the cold brook,

Candied with ice, caudle thy morning taste

To cure thy o'er-night's surfeit? Call the creatures

Whose naked natures live in all the spite

Of wreakful heaven, whose bare unhousèd trunks,

To the conflicting elements exposed,

Answer mere nature. Bid them flatter thee.

O thou shalt find —

              Timon.   A fool of thee. Depart.

Apemantus.   I love thee better now than e'er I did.

Timon.   I hate thee worse.

Apemantus.   Why?

Timon.	Thou flatter'st misery.
Apemantus.	I flatter not, but say thou art a caitiff.
Timon.	Why dost thou seek me out?
Apemantus.	To vex thee.
Timon.	Always a villain's office or a fool's.
	Dost please thyself in't?
Apemantus.	Ay.
Timon.	What, a knave too?
Apemantus.	If thou didst put this sour cold habit on

To castigate thy pride, 'twere well; but thou
Dost it enforcedly. Thou'dst courtier be again
Wert thou not beggar. Willing misery
Outlives incertain pomp, is crowned before.
The one is filling still, never complete;
The other, at high wish. Best state, contentless,
Hath a distracted and most wretched being,
Worse than the worst, content.
Thou shouldst desire to die, being miserable.

Timon. Not by his breath that is more miserable.
Thou art a slave, whom Fortune's tender arm

With favor never clasped, but bred a dog.
Hadst thou, like us, from our first swath proceeded
The sweet degrees that this brief world affords
To such as may the passive drudges of it
Freely command, thou wouldst have plunged thyself
In general riot, melted down thy youth
In different beds of lust, and never learned
The icy precepts of respect, but followed
The sug'red game before thee. But myself—
Who had the world as my confectionary,
The mouths, the tongues, the eyes, and hearts of men
At duty, more than I could frame employment;
That numberless upon me stuck, as leaves
Do on the oak, have with one winter's brush
Fell from their boughs, and left me open, bare
For every storm that blows—I to bear this,
That never knew but better, is some burden.
Thy nature did commence in sufferance, time
Hath made thee hard in't. Why shouldst thou hate men?
They never flattered thee. What hast thou given?

If thou wilt curse, thy father, that poor rogue,
Must be thy subject; who in spite put stuff
To some she-beggar and compounded thee
Poor rogue hereditary. Hence, begone.
If thou hadst not been born the worst of men,
Thou hadst been a knave and flatterer.

Apemantus.   Art thou proud yet?

Timon.   Ay, that I am not thee.

Apemantus.   I, that I was
No prodigal.

Timon.   I, that I am one now.
Were all the wealth I have shut up in thee,
I'd give thee leave to hang it. Get thee gone.
That the whole life of Athens were in this!
Thus would I eat it.

      [*Eats a root*]

Apemantus.   Here, I will mend thy feast.

      [*Offers him food*]

Timon.   First mend my company, take away thyself.

Apemantus.   So I shall mend mine own, by th' lack of thine.

Timon.	'Tis not well mended so, it is but botched;
	If not, I would it were.
Apemantus.	What wouldst thou have to Athens?
Timon.	Thee thither in a whirlwind. If thou wilt,
	Tell them there I have gold; look, so I have.
Apemantus.	Here is no use for gold.
Timon.	The best and truest;
	For here it sleeps and does no hirèd harm.
Apemantus.	Where liest a nights, Timon?
Timon.	Under that's above me.
	Where feed'st thou a days, Apemantus?
Apemantus.	Where my stomach finds meat, or rather where I eat it.
Timon.	Would poison were obedient and knew my mind!
Apemantus.	Where wouldst thou send it?
Timon.	To sauce thy dishes.
Apemantus.	The middle of humanity thou never knewest, but the extremity of both ends. When thou wast in thy gilt and thy perfume, they mocked thee for too much curiosity; in thy rags thou know'st none, but art despised for the contrary. There's a medlar for

           thee; eat it.

Timon. On what I hate I feed not.

Apemantus. Dost hate a medlar?

Timon. Ay, though it look like thee.

Apemantus. And th'hadst hated meddlers sooner, thou shouldst
have loved thyself better now. What man didst thou
ever know unthrift that was beloved after his means?

Timon. Who, without those means thou talk'st of, didst
thou ever know beloved?

Apemantus. Myself.

Timon. I understand thee; thou hadst some means to keep
a dog.

Apemantus. What things in the world canst thou nearest com-
pare to thy flatterers?

Timon. Women nearest, but men—men are the things
themselves. What wouldst thou do with the world,
Apemantus, if it lay in thy power?

Apemantus. Give it the beasts, to be rid of the men.

Timon. Wouldst thou have thyself fall in the confusion of
men, and remain a beast with the beasts?

Apemantus. Ay, Timon.

Timon. A beastly ambition, which the gods grant thee t' attain to. If thou wert the lion, the fox would beguile thee. If thou wert the lamb, the fox would eat thee. If thou wert the fox, the lion would suspect thee, when peradventure thou wert accused by the ass. If thou wert the ass, thy dullness would torment thee, and still thou liv'dst but as a breakfast to the wolf. If thou wert the wolf, thy greediness would afflict thee, and oft thou shouldst hazard thy life for thy dinner. Wert thou the unicorn, pride and wrath would confound thee, and make thine own self the conquest of thy fury. Wert thou a bear, thou wouldst be killed by the horse. Wert thou a horse, thou wouldst be seized by the leopard. Wert thou a leopard, thou wert german to the lion, and the spots of thy kindred were jurors on thy life. All thy safety were remotion, and thy defense absence. What beast couldst thou be that were not subject to a beast? And what a beast art thou already, that seest not thy loss in transformation!

Apemantus. If thou couldst please me with speaking to me, thou mightst have hit upon it here. The commonwealth of Athens is become a forest of beasts.

Timon. How has the ass broke the wall, that thou art out of the city?

Apemantus. Yonder comes a poet and a painter. The plague of company light upon thee! I will fear to catch it, and give way. When I know not what else to do, I'll see thee again.

Timon. When there is nothing living but thee, thou shalt be welcome. I had rather be a beggar's dog than Apemantus.

Apemantus. Thou art the cap of all the fools alive.

Timon. Would thou wert clean enough to spit upon.

Apemantus. A plague on thee, thou art too bad to curse.

Timon. All villains that do stand by thee are pure.

Apemantus. There is no leprosy but what thou speak'st.

Timon. If I name thee.
I'll beat thee, but I should infect my hands.

Apemantus.	I would my tongue could rot them off.
Timon.	Away, thou issue of a mangy dog.
	Choler does kill me that thou art alive;
	I swound to see thee.
Apemantus.	Would thou wouldst burst.
Timon.	Away, thou tedious rogue, I am sorry I shall lose a stone by thee.

        [*Throws a stone at him*]

Apemantus.	Beast!
Timon.	Slave!
Apemantus.	Toad!
Timon.	Rogue, rogue, rogue!
	I am sick of this false world, and will love naught
	But even the mere necessities upon't.
	Then, Timon, presently prepare thy grave.
	Lie where the light foam of the sea may beat
	Thy gravestone daily. Make thine epitaph,
	That death in me at others' lives may laugh.
	[*To the gold*] O thou sweet king-killer, and dear divorce
	'Twixt natural son and sire, thou bright defiler
	Of Hymen's purest bed, thou valiant Mars,

Thou ever young, fresh, loved, and delicate wooer,
Whose blush doth thaw the consecrated snow
That lies on Dian's lap. Thou visible god,
That sold'rest close impossibilities
And mak'st them kiss; that speak'st with every tongue
To every purpose. O thou touch of hearts,
Think thy slave man rebels, and by the virtue
Set them into confounding odds, that beasts
May have the world in empire.

Apemantus.   Would 'twere so,
But not till I am dead. I'll say th'hast gold.
Thou wilt be thronged to shortly.

Timon.   Thronged to?

Apemantus.   Ay.

Timon. Thy back, I prithee.

Apemantus.   Live, and love thy misery.

Timon. Long live so, and so die. I am quit.
          [*Enter the Banditti*]

Apemantus. Moe things like men! Eat, Timon, and abhor them.
          [*Exit Apemantus*]

First Bandit. Where should he have this gold! It is some poor fragment, some slender ort of his remainder. The mere want of gold, and the falling-from of his friends, drove him into this melancholy.

Second Bandit. It is noised he hath a mass of treasure.

Third Bandit. Let us make the assay upon him. If he care not for't, he will supply us easily; if he covetously reserve it, how shall's get it?

Second Bandit. True, for he bears it not about him; 'tis hid.

First Bandit. Is not this he?

All. Where?

Second Bandit. 'Tis his description.

Third Bandit. He? I know him.

All. Save thee, Timon.

Timon. Now, thieves?

All. Soldiers, not thieves.

Timon.   Both too, and women's sons.

All. We are not thieves, but men that much do want.

Timon. Your greatest want is, you want much of meat.
      Why should you want? Behold, the earth hath roots;

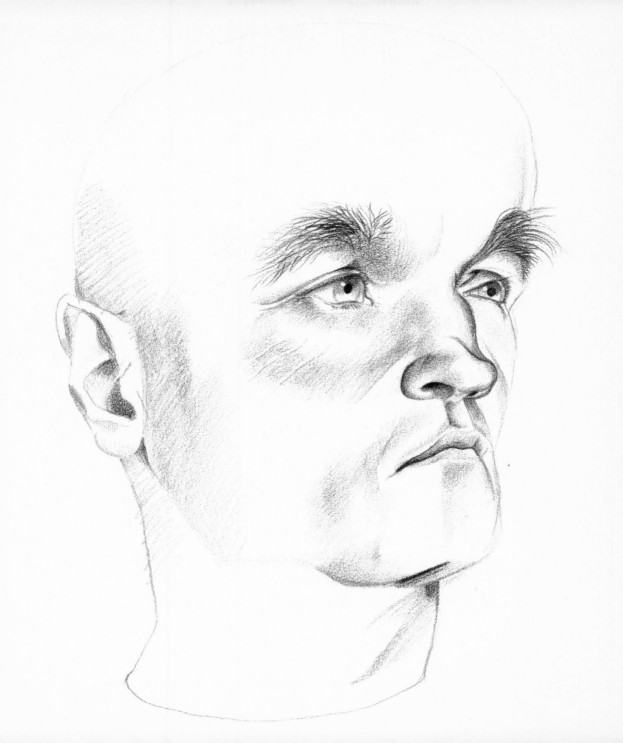

Within this mile break forth a hundred springs;
The oaks bear mast, the briers scarlet hips;
The bounteous huswife nature on each bush
Lays her full mess before you. Want? Why want?

First Bandit.   We cannot live on grass, on berries, water,
As beasts and birds and fishes.

Timon.   Nor on the beasts themselves, the birds and fishes;
You must eat men. Yet thanks I must you con
That you are thieves professed, that you work not
In holier shapes; for there is boundless theft
In limited professions. Rascal thieves,
Here's gold. Go, suck the subtle blood o' th' grape,
Till the high fever seethe your blood to froth,
And so 'scape hanging. Trust not the physician;
His antidotes are poison, and he slays
Moe than you rob. Take wealth and lives together,
Do, villain, do, since you protest to do't.
Like workmen, I'll example you with thievery:
The sun's a thief, and with his great attraction
Robs the vast sea. The moon's an arrant thief,

And her pale fire she snatches from the sun.
The sea's a thief, whose liquid surge resolves
The moon into salt tears. The earth's a thief,
That feeds and breeds by a composture stol'n
From gen'ral excrement. Each thing's a thief.
The laws, your curb and whip, in their rough power
Has unchecked theft. Love not yourselves; away,
Rob one another. There's more gold; cut throats,
All that you meet are thieves. To Athens go,
Break open shops; nothing can you steal
But thieves do lose it. Steal less for this I give you,
And gold confound you howsoe'er. Amen.

Third Bandit. Has almost charmed me from my profession
by persuading me to it.

First Bandit. 'Tis in the malice of mankind that he thus advises us,
not to have us thrive in our mystery.

Second Bandit. I'll believe him as an enemy, and give over my trade.

First Bandit. Let us first see peace in Athens; there is no time
so miserable but a man may be true.

  [*Exit Thieves*]

[Enter Flavius, the Steward to Timon]

Flavius.   O you gods!

Is yond despised and ruinous man my lord?

Full of decay and failing? O monument

And wonder of good deeds evilly bestowed!

What an alteration of honor has desp'rate want made!

What vilder thing upon the earth than friends,

Who can bring noblest minds to basest ends!

How rarely does it meet with this time's guise,

When man was wished to love his enemies!

Grant I may ever love, and rather woo

Those that would mischief me than those that do.

Has caught me in his eye; I will present

My honest grief unto him, and as my lord

Still serve him with my life. My dearest master.

Timon.   Away! What art thou?

Flavius.   Have you forgot me, sir?

Timon.   Why dost ask that? I have forgot all men.

Then, if thou grunt'st th'art a man,

I have forgot thee.

Flavius. An honest poor servant of yours.

Timon. Then I know thee not.
    I never had honest man about me, I; all
    I kept were knaves, to serve in meat to villains.

Flavius. The gods are witness,
    Nev'r did poor steward wear a truer grief
    For his undone lord than mine eyes for you.

Timon. What, dost thou weep? Come nearer. Then I love thee
    Because thou art a woman, and disclaim'st
    Flinty mankind, whose eyes do never give
    But thorough lust and laughter. Pity's sleeping.
    Strange times, that weep with laughing, not with weeping!

Flavius. I beg of you to know me, good my lord,
    T' accept my grief, and whilst this poor wealth lasts,
    To entertain me as your steward still.

Timon. Had I a steward
    So true, so just, and now so comfortable?
    It almost turns my dangerous nature mild.
    Let me behold thy face. Surely, this man
    Was born of woman.

Forgive my general and exceptless rashness,
You perpetual-sober gods. I do proclaim
One honest man. Mistake me not, but one.
No more I pray—and he's a steward.
How fain would I have hated all mankind,
And thou redeem'st thyself. But all save thee
I fell with curses.
Methinks thou art more honest now than wise;
For, by oppressing and betraying me,
Thou might'st have sooner got another service.
For many so arrive at second masters
Upon their first lord's neck. But tell me true—
For I must ever doubt, though ne'er so sure—
Is not thy kindness subtle, covetous,
A usuring kindness, as rich men deal gifts,
Expecting in return twenty for one?

Flavius. No, my most worthy master, in whose breast
Doubt and suspect, alas, are placed too late.
You should have feared false times when you did feast.
Suspect still comes where an estate is least.

That which I show, heaven knows, is merely love,
Duty and zeal to your unmatchèd mind,
Care of your food and living; and believe it,
My most honored lord,
For any benefit that points to me,
Either in hope or present, I'd exchange
For this one wish, that you had power and wealth
To requite me by making rich yourself.

Timon. Look thee, 'tis so. Thou singly honest man,
Here, take. The gods out of my misery
Has sent thee treasure. Go, live rich and happy,
But thus conditioned: thou shalt build from men;
Hate all, curse all, show charity to none,
But let the famished flesh slide from the bone
Ere thou relieve the beggar. Give to dogs
What thou deniest to men. Let prisons swallow 'em,
Debts wither 'em to nothing; be men like blasted woods,
And may diseases lick up their false bloods.
And so farewell, and thrive.

Flavius. O let me stay and comfort you, my master.

Timon.   If thou hat'st curses
Stay not; fly, whilst thou art blessed and free.
Ne'er see thou man, and let me ne'er see thee.

     [*Exit Flavius; and exit Timon into his cave*]

ACT FIVE

BEFORE TIMON'S CAVE

*[Enter Poet and Painter; Timon
listens from his cave, unseen]*

Painter. As I took note of the place, it cannot be far where he abides.

Poet. What's to be thought of him? Does the rumor hold for true that he's so full of gold?

Painter. Certain. Alcibiades reports it. Phrynia and Timandra had gold of him. He likewise enriched poor straggling soldiers with great quantity. 'Tis said he gave unto his steward a mighty sum.

Poet. Then this breaking of his has been but a try for his friends?

Painter. Nothing else. You shall see him a palm in Athens again, and flourish with the highest. Therefore 'tis not amiss we tender our loves to him in this supposed distress of his. It will show honestly in us, and is very likely to load our purposes with what they travail for, if it be a just and true report that goes of his having.

Poet.   What have you now to present unto him?

Painter.   Nothing at this time but my visitation; only I will promise him an excellent piece.

Poet.   I must serve him so too, tell him of an intent that's coming toward him.

Painter.   Good as the best. Promising is the very air o' th' time; it opens the eyes of expectation. Performance is ever the duller for his act, and but in the plainer and simpler kind of people, the deed of saying is quite out of use. To promise is most courtly and fashionable; performance is a kind of will or testament, which argues a great sickness in his judgment that makes it.

                    [*Enter Timon from his cave*]

Timon.   [*Aside*] Excellent workman, thou canst not paint a man so bad as is thyself.

Poet.   I am thinking what I shall say I have provided for him. It must be a personating of himself; a satire against the softness of prosperity, with a discovery of the infinite flatteries that follow youth and opulency.

Timon.   *[Aside]* Must thou needs stand for a villain in thine
own work? Wilt thou whip thine own faults in other
men? Do so, I have gold for thee.

Poet.   Nay, let's seek him.
Then do we sin against our own estate,
When we may profit meet, and come too late.

Painter.   True.
When the day serves, before black-cornered night,
Find what thou want'st by free and offered light.
Come.

Timon.   *[Aside]* I'll meet you at the turn.
What a god's gold, that he is worshiped
In a baser temple than where swine feed!
'Tis thou that rig'st the bark and plough'st the foam,
Settlest admirèd reverence in a slave.
To thee be worshiped and thy saints for aye;
Be crowned with plagues that thee alone obey.
Fit I meet them.
     [Comes forward]

Poet.   Hail, worthy Timon.

Painter   Our late noble master.

Timon. Have I once lived to see two honest men?

Poet. Sir,

Having often of your open bounty tasted,

Hearing you were retired, your friends fall'n off,

Whose thankless natures, O abhorrèd spirits,

Not all the whips of heaven are large enough—

What, to you,

Whose star-like nobleness gave life and influence

To their whole being! I am rapt, and cannot cover

The monstrous bulk of this ingratitude

With any size of words.

Timon.   Let it go;

Naked, men may see't the better.

You that are honest, by being what you are,

Make them best seen and known.

Painter.   He and myself

Have traveled in the great show'r of your gifts,

And sweetly felt it.

Timon.   Ay, you are honest men.

Painter.	We are hither come to offer you our service.
Timon.	Most honest men. Why, how shall I requite you?
	Can you eat roots and drink cold water? No?
Both.	What we can do, we'll do to do you service.
Timon.	Y'are honest men. Y'have heard that I have gold,
	I am sure you have. Speak truth, y'are honest men.
Painter.	So it is said, my noble lord, but therefore
	Came not my friend nor I.
Timon.	Good honest men. Thou draw'st a counterfeit
	Best in all Athens. Th'art indeed the best;
	Thou counterfeit'st most lively.
Painter.	So-so, my lord.
Timon.	E'en so, sir, as I say. And for thy fiction,
	Why thy verse swells with stuff so fine and smooth
	That thou art even natural in thine art.
	But for all this, my honest-natured friends,
	I must needs say you have a little fault;
	Marry, 'tis not monstrous in you, neither wish I
	You take much pains to mend.
Both.	Beseech your honor

To make it known to us.

Timon.   You'll take it ill.

Both. Most thankfully, my lord.

Timon.   Will you indeed?

Both. Doubt it not, worthy lord.

Timon. There's never a one of you but trusts a knave
That mightily deceives you.

Both.   Do we, my lord?

Timon. Ay, and you hear him cog, see him dissemble,
Know his gross patchery, love him, feed him,
Keep in your bosom, yet remain assured
That he's a made-up villain.

Painter. I know none such, my lord.

Poet.   Nor I.

Timon. Look you, I love you well; I'll give you gold:
Rid me these villains from your companies.
Hang them, or stab them, drown them in a draught,
Confound them by some course, and come to me,
I'll give you gold enough.

Both. Name them, my lord, let's know them.

Timon.   You that way, and you this; but two in company.
Each man apart, all single and alone,
Yet an arch-villain keeps him company.
[*To one*] If where thou art, two villains shall not be,
Come not near him. [*To the other*] If thou wouldst not reside
But where one villain is, then him abandon.
Hence, pack, there's gold; you came for gold, ye slaves.
[*To one*] You have work for me, there's payment.
Hence!
[*To the other*] You are an alchemist, make gold of that.
Out, rascal dogs!

     [*Beats them out, then retires into his cave*]

     [*Enter Flavius, the Steward, and two Senators*]

Flavius.   It is vain that you would speak with Timon,
For he is set so only to himself
That nothing but himself, which looks like man,
Is friendly with him.

First Senator.   Bring us to his cave.
It is our part and promise to th' Athenians
To speak with Timon.

Second Senator.   At all times alike
Men are not still the same; 'twas time and griefs
That framed him thus. Time with his fairer hand
Offering the fortunes of his former days,
The former man may make him. Bring us to him,
And chance it as it may.

Flavius.   Here is his cave.
Peace and content be here. Lord Timon! Timon!
Look out, and speak to friends. Th' Athenians
By two of their most reverend senate greet thee.
Speak to them, noble Timon.

            [Enter Timon out of his cave]

Timon.   Thou sun that comforts, burn! Speak and be hanged.
For each true word a blister, and each false
Be as a cauterizing to the root o' th' tongue,
Consuming it with speaking.

First Senator.   Worthy Timon—

Timon.   Of none but such as you, and you of Timon.

First Senator.   The senators of Athens greet thee, Timon.

Timon.   I thank them, and would send them back the plague,

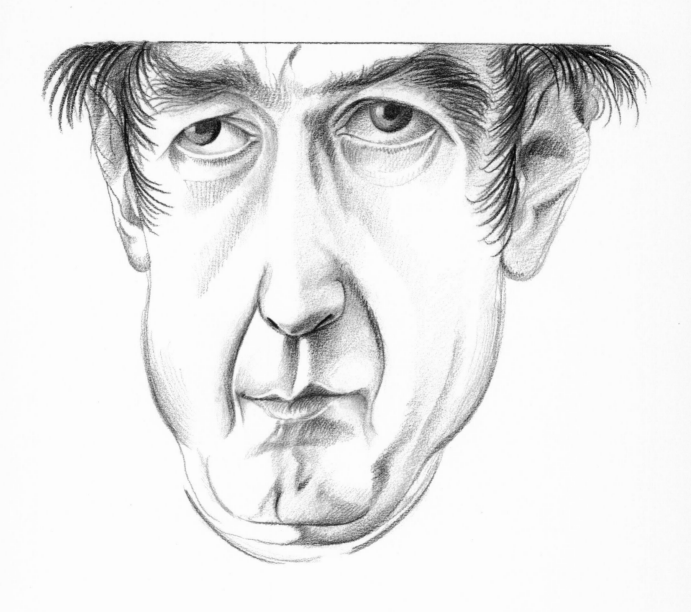

Could I but catch it for them.

First Senator.   O forget

What we are sorry for ourselves in thee.

The senators, with one consent of love,

Entreat thee back to Athens, who have thought

On special dignities, which vacant lie

For thy best use and wearing.

Second Senator.   They confess

Toward thee forgetfulness too general gross;

Which now the public body, which doth seldom

Play the recanter, feeling in itself

A lack of Timon's aid, hath sense withal

Of it own fall, restraining aid to Timon;

And send forth us to make their sorrowed render,

Together with a recompense more fruitful

Than their offense can weigh down by the dram —

Ay, even such heaps and sums of love and wealth

As shall to thee blot out what wrongs were theirs,

And write in thee the figures of their love,

Ever to read them thine.

Timon.   You witch me in it;
Surprise me to the very brink of tears.
Lend me a fool's heart and a woman's eyes,
And I'll beweep these comforts, worthy senators.

First Senator. Therefore so please thee to return with us,
And of our Athens, thine and ours, to take
The captainship, thou shalt be met with thanks,
Allowed with absolute power, and thy good name
Live with authority. So soon we shall drive back
Of Alcibiades th' approaches wild,
Who like a boar too savage doth root up
His country's peace.

Second Senator.   And shakes his threat'ning sword
Against the walls of Athens.

First Senator.   Therefore, Timon —

Timon. Well, sir, I will; therefore I will, sir, thus:
If Alcibiades kill my countrymen,
Let Alcibiades know this of Timon,
That Timon cares not. But if he sack fair Athens,
And take our goodly agèd men by th' beards,

Giving our holy virgins to the stain

Of contumelious, beastly, mad-brained war,

Then let him know, and tell him Timon speaks it,

In pity of our agèd and our youth,

I cannot choose but tell him that I care not,

And let him take't at worst. For their knives care not

While you have throats to answer. For myself,

There's not a whittle in th' unruly camp

But I do prize it at my love before

The reverend'st throat in Athens. So I leave you

To the protection of the prosperous gods,

As thieves to keepers.

Flavius.   Stay not, all's in vain.

Timon.   Why I was writing of my epitaph;

It will be seen tomorrow. My long sickness

Of health and living now begins to mend,

And nothing brings me all things. Go, live still;

Be Alcibiades your plague, you his,

And last so long enough.

First Senator.   We speak in vain.

Timon.   But yet I love my country, and am not
One that rejoices in the common wrack,
As common bruit doth put it.

First Senator.   That's well spoke.

Timon.   Commend me to my loving countrymen.

First Senator.   These words become your lips as they pass thorough them.

Second Senator.   And enter in our ears like great triumphers
In their applauding gates.

Timon.   Commend me to them,
And tell them that to ease them of their griefs,
Their fears of hostile strokes, their aches, losses,
Their pangs of love, with other incident throes
That nature's fragile vessel doth sustain
In life's uncertain voyage, I will some kindness do them;
I'll teach them to prevent wild Alcibiades' wrath.

First Senator.   I like this well; he will return again.

Timon.   I have a tree which grows here in my close,
That mine own use invites me to cut down,
And shortly must I fell it. Tell my friends,
Tell Athens, in the sequence of degree,

From high to low throughout, that whoso please
To stop affliction, let him take his haste;
Come hither ere my tree hath felt the ax,
And hang himself. I pray you do my greeting.

Flavius. Trouble him no further; thus you still shall find him.

Timon. Come not to me again, but say to Athens,
Timon hath made his everlasting mansion
Upon the beachèd verge of the salt flood,
Who once a day with his embossèd froth
The turbulent surge shall cover. Thither come,
And let my gravestone be your oracle.
Lips, let four words go by and language end.
What is amiss, plague and infection mend.
Graves only be men's works and death their gain.
Sun, hide thy beams; Timon hath done his reign.

　　　　[*Exit Timon*]

First Senator. His discontents are unremovably
Coupled to nature.

Second Senator. Our hope in him is dead. Let us return,
And strain what other means is left unto us

In our dear peril.

First Senator.   It requires swift foot.

[*Exeunt*]

BEFORE THE WALLS OF ATHENS

[Enter two other Senators with a Messenger]

Third Senator. Thou hast painfully discovered. Are his files
As full as thy report?

Messenger.   I have spoke the least.
Besides, his expedition promises
Present approach.

Fourth Senator. We stand much hazard if they bring not Timon.

Messenger. I met a courier, one mine ancient friend,
Whom though in general part we were opposed,
Yet our old love made a particular force,
And made us speak like friends. This man was riding
From Alcibiades to Timon's cave
With letters of entreaty, which imported
His fellowship i' th' cause against your city,
In part for his sake moved.

[Enter the other Senators from Timon]

Third Senator.   Here come our brothers.

First Senator. No talk of Timon, nothing of him expect.

The enemy's drum is heard, and fearful scouring
Doth choke the air with dust. In, and prepare.
Ours is the fall, I fear, our foes the snare.
      {*Exeunt*}

BEFORE TIMON'S CAVE

[Enter a Soldier in the woods, seeking Timon]

Soldier. By all description this should be the place.
Who's here? Speak, ho! No answer? What is this?
"Timon is dead, who hath outstretched his span.
Some beast read this; there does not live a man."
Dead, sure, and this his grave. What's on this tomb
I cannot read. The character I'll take with wax;
Our captain hath in every figure skill,
An aged interpreter, though young in days.
Before proud Athens he's set down by this,
Whose fall the mark of his ambition is.

　　　[Exit]

BEFORE THE WALLS OF ATHENS

[Trumpets sound. Enter Alcibiades
with his powers before Athens]

Alcibiades.   Sound to this coward and lascivious town
Our terrible approach.

[Sounds a parley]

[The Senators appear upon the walls]

Till now you have gone on, and filled the time
With all licentious measure, making your wills
The scope of justice. Till now, myself and such
As slept within the shadow of your power,
Have wandered with our traversed arms and breathed
Our sufferance vainly. Now the time is flush,
When crouching marrow in the bearer strong
Cries, of itself, "No more." Now breathless wrong
Shall sit and pant in your great chairs of ease,
And pursy insolence shall break his wind
With fear and horrid flight.

First Senator.   Noble and young,

When thy first griefs were but a mere conceit,
Ere thou hadst power or we had cause of fear,
We sent to thee to give thy rages balm,
To wipe out our ingratitude with loves
Above their quantity.

Second Senator.   So did we woo
Transformèd Timon to our city's love
By humble message and by promised means.
We were not all unkind, nor all deserve
The common stroke of war.

First Senator.   These walls of ours
Were not erected by their hands from whom
You have received your grief; nor are they such
That these great tow'rs, trophies, and schools should fall
For private faults in them.

Second Senator.   Nor are they living
Who were the motives that you first went out.
Shame that they wanted cunning in excess
Hath broke their hearts. March, noble lord,
Into our city with thy banners spread.

By decimation and tithèd death,
If thy revenges hunger for that food
Which nature loathes, take thou the destined tenth,
And by the hazard of the spotted die,
Let die the spotted.

First Senator.   All have not offended.
For those that were, it is not square to take
On those that are, revenge. Crimes, like lands,
Are not inherited. Then, dear countryman,
Bring in thy ranks, but leave without thy rage.
Spare thy Athenian cradle and those kin
Which in the bluster of thy wrath must fall
With those that have offended. Like a shepherd,
Approach the fold and cull th' infected forth,
But kill not all together.

Second Senator.   What thou wilt,
Thou rather shalt enforce it with thy smile
Than hew to't with thy sword.

First Senator.   Set but thy foot
Against our rampired gates, and they shall ope,

So thou wilt send thy gentle heart before
To say thou't enter friendly.

Second Senator.   Throw thy glove,
Or any token of thine honor else,
That thou wilt use the wars as thy redress
And not as our confusion. All thy powers
Shall make their harbor in our town till we
Have sealed thy full desire.

Alcibiades.   Then there's my glove.
Descend and open your uncharged ports.
Those enemies of Timon's and mine own
Whom you yourselves shall set out for reproof,
Fall, and no more. And to atone your fears
With my more noble meaning, not a man
Shall pass his quarter, or offend the stream
Of regular justice in your city's bounds,
But shall be remedied to your public laws
At heaviest answer.

Both Senators.   'Tis most nobly spoken.
Alcibiades.   Descend, and keep your words.

[The Senators descend, and open the gates]

[Enter a Soldier]

Soldier. My noble general, Timon is dead,
Entombed upon the very hem o' th' sea,
And on his gravestone this insculpture which
With wax I brought away, whose soft impression
Interprets for my poor ignorance.

[Alcibiades reads the epitaph]

Alcibiades. "Here lies a wretched corse, of wretched soul bereft.
Seek not my name. A plague consume you, wicked caitiffs left.
Here lie I, Timon, who alive all living men did hate.
Pass by and curse thy fill, but pass, and stay not here thy gait."
These well express in thee thy latter spirits.
Though thou abhorr'dst in us our human griefs,
Scorn'dst our brains' flow, and those our droplets which
From niggard nature fall; yet rich conceit
Taught thee to make vast Neptune weep for aye
On thy low grave, on faults forgiven. Dead
Is noble Timon, of whose memory
Hereafter more. Bring me into your city,

And I will use the olive with my sword,
Make war breed peace, make peace stint war, make each
Prescribe to other, as each other's leech.
Let our drums strike.

    [*Exeunt*]

FINIS

COLOPHON

Typography by Royal Composing Room, Inc.
The text is photocomposed in 14 pt. Cloister
with 12 pt. Cloister Italic and 9 pt. Cloister Bold.
The display copy is Photo Display Cloister Bold.
Complete page negatives were prepared for platemaking.
Printed Lithography by Rae Publishing Co., Inc.
The paper, manufactured by Finch, Pruyn & Company, Inc.,
is Finch Opaque, Vellum Finish, Cream White, Basis 80.
Binding by A. Horowitz & Sons/Bookbinders, with
Holliston Cloth and Rainbow Antique endpapers.
Typographic coordination by Irving Levine.
Illustrations by Isadore Seltzer.
Design by Daniel Haberman.

WILLIAM SHAKESPEARE:
THE LIFE OF TIMON OF ATHENS